★ ★ ★ Important Announcement, page 1 ★ ★ ★

The Mystery Fancier

Volume 4 Number 5
September/October 1980

THE MYSTERY FANCIER

Volume 4 Number 5
September/October, 1980

TABLE OF CONTENTS

```
MYSTERIOUSLY SPEAKING . . . . . . . . . . . . . . . . . . . . . 1
The Apocryphalization of Holmes, by E.F. Bleiler. . . . . . . 3
Edwin's Mystery and Its History, by Ben Fisher. . . . . . . . 6
THE LINE-UP, by Walter Albert . . . . . . . . . . . . . . . . 9
I Remember.... B-Movies, by Jeff Banks. . . . . . . . . . . . 13
Old Time Radio Lives, by Carl Larsen. . . . . . . . . . . . . 18
Spy Series Characters in Hardback, Part IV,
   by Barry Van Tilburg. . . . . . . . . . . . . . . . . . . 21
IT'S ABOUT CRIME, by Marvin Lachman . . . . . . . . . . . . . 24
MYSTERY*FILE: Short Reviews by Steve Lewis. . . . . . . . . . 27
VERDICTS (More Reviews) . . . . . . . . . . . . . . . . . . . 37
THE DOCUMENTS IN THE CASE (Letters) . . . . . . . . . . . . . 44
```

The MYSTERY FANcier
(USPS:428-590)
is edited and published bi-monthly by Guy M. Townsend,
840 East Main Street, #5, Blytheville, Arkansas 72315.
Contributions of all descriptions are welcomed.

SUBSCRIPTION RATES: Domestic second class mail, $9.00 per year (6 issues); overseas surface mail, $9.00; overseas airmail, $12.00. Overseas subscribers please pay in international money order, check drawn on U.S. bank, or currency; no checks drawn on foreign banks, please.

Second class postage paid at Blytheville, Arkansas

Copyright 1980 by Guy M. Townsend
All rights reserved for contributors
ISSN:0146-3160

MYSTERIOUSLY SPEAKING...

All right, folks, pay attention. At the beginning of this volume I mentioned that the price would have to be raised for volume 5--if, indeed, I didn't just give the magazine up altogether. Those of you who have had no experience putting out a magazine like this can have no idea whatever of the amount of time and labor it entails. I'm not complaining about that—if I didn't think it was worthwhile and didn't derive some enjoyment from it, I just wouldn't do it. But it's one thing to have a hobby which eats huge holes in your spare time, and quite another to have a hobby which also eats huge holes in your pocket book, which is what TMF has done to me since it was first begun, and it's gotten worse every year.

Until now, looking forward to a steady expansion in readership, I have had an excessive number of issues printed over the actual number of subscribers. At the end of each year, TMF's subscription list totals about 225 (including twenty or so publishers who get their copies free, and fifty or more subscribers who pay reduced subscription rates in totally inadequate recompense for their contributions to these pages). Altogether, TMF generally has the equivalent of about 175 full-price subscribers, which means that I bring in about $1575 a year in subscriptions.

For the past couple of years I have been having 350 copies of each issue run off, at a cost--*for printing alone*--of about $250 per issue. That price, by the way, is the lowest I have been able to find anywhere around here, and in order to get it I have to drive two round trips of 150 miles each, the cost of which is not included in that figure. Locally, I have been quoted prices as high as $450 per issue.

Part of the cost is for the superfluous copies of TMF which I have been having printed. I could get by with 250 copies, instead of 350, and still have a few spare copies left over each time, but reducing the number of copies by roughly a third would not effect savings of nearly that amount. The more copies you print, the cheaper the additional copies are. In fact, cutting back to 250 probably would not produce a saving of much more than 10%.

The cost of the last issue of TMF (4:4), including printing costs, second class mailing fees, envelopes, transportation, and odds and ends, probably ran right at $450, which means that I spent almost $200 more on that issue than I actually took in in subscriptions. Admittedly, that issue was more expensive than normal, since I had some unusual expenses --such as a fee for transferring the second class mailing permit--but I have been losing a good $50 to $100 per issue ever since this magazine went offset, and it simply has got to stop.

It is obvious that I cannot break even at the current $9 rate, but if I raise the subscription rate to $12 and cut back on surplus issues, I think I can break even on a print run of 150 with as few as 100 full fare subscribers. That is, I think I can cover the cost of producing 150 copies of each issue for $200 per issue, which is what 100 subscriptions at $12 per would bring in each year.

So what I am going to do is to ask you all to declare yourselves, *within two weeks of receiving this issue,* as to whether you will be willing to subscribe to TMF volume 5 for $12. (Overseas air mail will go to $15, and overseas surface will rise to $12.) Just send me a postcard saying yes, and you can deduct the ten cents it costs you from the $12 if you wish. If I get at least 100 commitments, TMF will continue; if I get 99 or fewer, volume 4, number 6, will be the last issue of TMF ever printed.

I am sure a good many of you will choose not to renew at the higher rate. There has been a good bit of bitching in the past about the high subscription cost of TMF, and I imagine some of you will think it is unreasonable of me to ask that you pay $12 for your subscription. But *my* subscription costs me hundreds of dollars each year--not to mention hundreds of hours of unpaid labor--and, frankly, I'd rather not hear from those of you who aren't willing to shell out the cost of one good restaurant meal to continue getting TMF.

To end on a happy note, I am happy to say that the next issue of TMF will include a special Bouchercon section, complete with photographs. Between us, John Nieminski and I took several hundred photographs at the Washington gathering, and I will be incorporating as many of them as possible into TMF 4:6.

Meanwhile, let's be optimistic about the future and send those articles, reviews, and letters in to TMF. Even if TMF folds with 4:6 I'll try to get as many of them as possible into that issue, and any I don't use will be returned promptly

Let me hear from you soon, folks. It's up to you whether TMF goes on any longer, or calls it quits after four good years.

THE APOCRYPHALIZATION OF HOLMES
By E. F. Bleiler

Sherlock Holmes: The Published Apocrypha by Sir Arthur Conan Doyle and Associated Hands. Selected and Edited by Jack Tracy. Houghton Mifflin, 1980, $11.95.

    The word "apocrypha" can have several meanings, ranging from things so secret that they should not be revealed, to spurious matters. In this context it means items by A. Conan Doyle that are more or less concerned with Sherlock Holmes but are peripheral to the sixty short stories and novels.
    Mr. Tracy has assembled the Sherlockian apocrypha in a single very useful, very entertaining volume. The book begins with two short self-parodies by Doyle, "The Field Bazaar" and "How Watson Learned the Trick," the second of which is very amusing. Also present is J. M. Barrie's "Adventure of the Two Collaborators"; it is stretching things a little to include it, but it is still worth having for its biographical context. It was the by-product of an unsuccessful collaboration between Barrie and Doyle. Somewhat more tenuous as marginalia are "The Man with the Watches" and "The Lost Special," two stories from *Round the Fire*. These mention in passing the odd and aberrant solutions of an officious amateur. Some readers have taken these comments to be slighting references to Holmes by Doyle, but this could be argued. It is just as likely that they mirror Doyle's delight in the crank aspects of journalism, like agony columns and newspaper cryptograms.
    Most of Tracy's book is taken up with dramatic material. William Gillette's play *Sherlock Holmes* is present, and Tracy makes a good case for Doyle's having had a larger share in its creation than is usually recognized. Much cleverer, perhaps because it is not so ambitious, is Gillette's *Painful Predicament of Sherlock Holmes*, a short one-act farce. One could probably sit through this, but it would be only a rabid (or sleeping) fan who could sit through *Sherlock Holmes*, as I remember from the cut, camp version staged a few years ago.
    Much the most interesting components of this volume are two plays that Doyle himself wrote about Holmes. These are *The Speckled Band* and *The Crown Diamond*. It is good to have these, since *The Speckled Band* has long been out of print in the French's Acting Edition, and *The Crown Diamond* has never really been available. Its only other printing seems to have been a limited 59-copy edition put out by Edgar Smith in 1958. To me these two plays are more than worth the price of the book.
    Not that they are good plays. They are not. The best that can be said for them is that they are mediocre specimens of the late 19th century melodrama (despite their later dates of origin). Contemporary viewers and critics seem to have rated them low, but they are fascinating documents in showing the working of Doyle's mind.
    The Speckled Band is a conflation and redirection of the short story of the same title. Staged in 1910, published in 1912, it abandons the linear plot of the short story and centers around three stage situations. The play opens at Stoke Moran, where an inquest is being held on Violet Stonor,

whom Dr. Roylott has just murdered. The second scene of the
second act shifts to Baker Street, and the third act returns
to Stoke Moran. Watson is responsible for Holmes's entry into
the situation, for Watson has been a friend of the Stonors in
India. Dr. Roylott has a housekeeper-mistress who keeps badg-
ering him about marriage and an Indian Moslem servant who
tends to the snake. As foils to them are a lacrymose old
butler and a feisty groceryman. Holmes disguises himself as
a butler to gain entry to the house. And so on down to the
snake in the ventilator.

The real problem with the play is the obvious one. Only
a first-rate dramatist could have stretched a short story into
a stage piece that fills an evening, and Doyle was not up to
it. Padding, extraneous characters, stage stereotypes all
destroy the sharpness of the story line. Doyle was clever
enough in the short story to keep the unamiable doctor out of
sight most of the time. With prolonged exposure in the play
he is simply a rather fumbling bore. Only in one small point
is the play superior to the short story: Holmes does not
straighten out the poker.

Doyle's other play, *The Crown Diamond*, as Tracy points
out, is a prevision of "The Mazarin Stone," combined with
elements of "The Adventure of the Empty House." In it Holmes
sets up a wax bust in the bow window, hooks up an electric
alarm system, outwits Colonel Moran, and recoups the fabulous-
ly valuable stolen diamond.

The writing circumstances of *The Crown Diamond* are much
less clear than those of *The Speckled Band*. It surfaced in
May 1921, when it was performed once in Bristol and was then
shown desultorily in London up through August 1921 for a total
(according to Tracy) of 29 Performances. "The Mazarin Stone,"
which is much the same story, was then published in the
October 1921 issue of the *Strand* magazine.

This is indeed a curious publishing situation, and one can
only wonder at the timing of the two pieces. All sorts of
questions arise. Was the play intended as a publicity device
for the story, a device that did not work? Did the *Strand*
agree to the staging of the play on the understanding that
names would be changed, to avoid direct competition? Was
there no connection between the two events, beyond the fact
that Doyle sent both pieces out at about the same time? Is
the play an offshoot of the story, or is the story a refur-
bishing of the failed play? What did Doyle hope to accomplish
with so short a play, and had he completely lost his critical
sense?

Adrian Doyle, who examined the manuscript of the play
closely, judged, on the basis of handwriting and paper, that
the play must have been written much earlier than 1921. Since
Doyle never threw anything away, this situation is highly
probable. Inasmuch as the play shares elements with "The
Adventure of the Empty House," which was published in 1903,
Tracy feels that the play was the prototype and source of the
short story and was trunked after the story was written.

This is entirely possible, and I probably should not
speculate, since I am limited to the printed text. But I
wonder if the reverse dating may not be stronger. There are
two internal points that suggest a later date for the play
than 1902-1093. First is the gem itself. The story would
have milieu if it had been written during the excitement over

the discovery and cutting of the Cullinan diamond and its acquisition by the Crown. This took place between 1905 and 1907. Second, the play makes several references to Colonel Moran's airgun. Yet the gun does not appear and is not used. These references make little sense in vacuo as they stand, but if a reader already knew of the colonel's b.b. gun from "The Adventure of the Empty House," the background of the play would be enhanced. If these speculations are correct, the play might be dated at 1906.

The last item of importance in Tracy's collection is "The Case of the Man Who Was Wanted," which was presented with great fanfare back in the 1940's as a recently discovered story by Doyle. Those of us who are old enough to remember will also recall that it turned out to be an honest mistake. It was written by one Arthur Whitaker, who sold it to Doyle for reworking. Doyle never used it and Whitaker's typed sheets were found among Doyle's papers. In retrospect, as is always the case with such incidents, I can only marvel that Whitaker's clumsy writing could ever have been mistaken for Doyle's sharp, clear, brisk prose--but so it goes.

In addition to the works of Doyle (and colleagues) the reader will also get a series of full, clear, nicely written introductions by Tracy. All in all, I find this one of the few books in the recent Sherlock boom that really merit publication. Because of its almost unique contents it belongs in the collection of every serious student of the detective story.

EDWIN'S MYSTERY AND ITS HISTORY:
Or, Another Look at Datchery
By Ben Fisher

To supplement ideas offered by Everett F. Bleiler concern- the identity of Datchery in Dickens' *The Mystery of Edwin Drood*, I offer these observations of my own. Like Bleiler, I thought over these points some years ago, and offered terse comments upon them in the *Dickens Studies Newsletter* ["Paperback Editions of *The Mystery of Edwin Drood*," 8 (March, 1977): 19-22], but it seems high time to elaborate. Although I have always respected greatly Bleiler's work in the mystery-detective fiction field, and though I comprehend only too well the quicksands awaiting those who tread unwarily through the mysteries of *Drood*, and especially those centered in reading Dickens' manuscript, a scratched and blotted document, I believe that evidence points to identifying Dick Datchery with Mr. Grewgious' clerk, Bazzard. I think that Bleiler minimizes Bazzard's potential for acting, and I believe, too, that a section of the novel, long overlooked, bears out in terms of ordinary plotting, as well as in symbolic drift, Bazzard's being Datcher.

To attend more specifically Bleiler's thinking on pp. 10-11 of "The Dilemma of Datchery," I find that he does not sufficiently credit Bazzard's latent qualities. The dour clerk in Grewgious' offices, who seems altogether lacking in personality or richness of character "as he appears," to quote Bleiler, is not at that time in true form, nor does he willingly perform his services. Bleiler's "appears" may have unintentional ironies, particularly if we notice his remarks on "deliberate misdirection" by Dickens, presented in several subsequent paragraphs. Dickens may have deliberately misled readers, but he may have done so, with simultaneous clues about his lumpy clerk's importance, to take the heat off Bazzard as Datchery. Similar feats of confused identity had already appeared in such characters as Magwitch (*Great Expectations*) and Rokesmith or Boffin (*Our Mutual Friend*), and it would be no mighty wonder that he would try again, in a novel where confusion of identity ramifies throughout many levels of meaning and implication.

Moreover, role playing is of the essence in *Drood*, centered in the personage of John Jasper, hypocritical choirister and uncle to Edwin Drood, whom he wishes to murder in order to get lovely young Rosa Bud for himself. Jasper consciously adopts poses to suit his audience of the moment: he is the obsequious good young man with Mayor Sapsea (a guise that doesn't withstand the shrewder comprehension of Mr. Grewgious), and he masks as a genial host and peacemaker for Edwin Drood and Neville Landless (but we readers divine what Dickens genuinely intends to convey--that Jasper is a baddie), he the solicitous relative of Edwin when he stands before Crisparkle (but his underlying eroticism and violence are not lost upon Rosa and Helena--whose name significantly signifies "light," or what will unmask Jasper in the end). Miss Twinkleton, the schoolmistress, also exists in dual planes of personality. So does Durdles, the not altogether befuddled stonemason. So do the Princess Puffer, Deputy, Grewgious, Honeythunder, and the Landless twins. *Drood* indeed contains a veritable cast of "actors," so why relegate Bazzard to the shades?

For additional evidence I refer to the cover for the original monthly parts of the novel. In the center stands a circle of rose stems, the roses overshadowed by the thorns, which comprises a veritable crown. Dickens' attentiveness to his illustrators' lining up their graphics with his own propensities is well known, so much so that I doubt we can disregard the throny crown and its ramifications. At the bottom appear the shovel and key, plus Durdles' lunch packet--tools that would have proved useful in ferreting out the conclusion, had *Drood* been finished. "Key" and "rose" thus come to be terms laden with suggestion.

There is the scene in which Grewgious hands over to Edwin Rosa's mother's ring, a section of writing in which Dickens ties together several of these strands, and in which the function of Datchery has such apparent unimportance that previous commentators have passed it by. Formed into a rose, this engagement ring takes on symbolic qualities integral to the development of the novel. Fashioned of rubies and diamonds, the ring is intended for a girl named Rosa, or Rosebud, because of her youthful, virginal qualities. Her own mother's engagement ring, this gem links the past with the present. With this bond plus the cluster of names, it is difficult to suppose that Dickens didn't intend to highlight "roses" in later portions of his book, a book that breaks off just as the revelations of the past and its effects upon the characters begin to come our way. Not only is the rose motif important in the matter of the ring, it may have been tied to Bazzard's unpublished, unperformed play, "The Thorn of Anxiety," about which Grewgious is pointed in his conversation. Roses, thorns--literal or otherwise--and anxieties are very much parts of *The Mystery of Edwin Drood*.

We come now to the crucial passages, those in which Grewgious makes certain that his business is properly handled. He request Bazzard to view the ring he is giving over to Drood:

> "In discharge of a trust, I have handed Mr. Edwin Drood a ring of diamonds and rubies. You see?"
> Edwin reproduced the little case, and opened it; and Bazzard looked into it.
> "I follow you both, sir," returned Bazzard, "and I witness the transaction."*

---

* I quote the text edited by Arthur J. Cox for the Penguin English Library (1974). Cox has produced several studies indicating his familiarity with the original manuscript and its difficulties. The printed text of *Drood* stood uncorrected, although howlers exist in the opening lines (so often quoted as Dickens' style at its height!) and elsewhere to baffle readers for over a century. Certain differences may be worth checking in Margaret Cardwell's edition of *Drood*, prepared for the progressing Clarendon Edition of Dickens' works (1972). Even the text of this novel has afforded its share of devilment to the controversies raging round it. My own ideas on *Drood* as part detective novel, part great prose poem were delivered as the annual Birthday Dinner Speech to the Philadelphia Branch of the Dickens Fellowship on February 9, 1980.

Who better to understand the implications of that ring when, later, it would have loomed large--have been a "key"--in identifying the body and the murderer, as John Forster, Dickens' confidante and literary executor, stated that it would do? Thus, rose, ring, and key assume figurative dimensions of no mean proportions here.

Other than Grewgious and Edwin, Bazzard is the only character to know anything about the ring and its being in Drood's possession. Jasper, who has memorized the extend of Edwin's other jewellery, those pieces so incriminating to Neville when they are later discovered in the weir, knows nothing about the ring on Edwin's person that fatal Christmas Eve. That Bazzard is intended to "follow" both Drood and Grewgious may also be fraught with more-than-literal connotation in the passage cited above. *Drood* abounds in pursuits, or "followings," and counter-pursuits. I see no obstacle to thinking of Bazzard's being sent to Cloisterham by Grewgious to dog Jasper's footsteps, just as the latter worthy sets upon the comings and goings of Neville. As Dick Datchery, the disguized Bazzard might well have played variations on the "Thorn-of-Anziety" theme as he surveyed the circumstances of the choirmaster, tightening around him all the while nets like those Jasper himself had mentioned to Rosa as intended for Neville Landless--who has fallen in love with her.

In closing, I wish to make clear that, like Bleiler, I know full well how easy is the "clouding" of others' arguments. That I have not attempted. The links among roses, keys, role-playing, and identity seem to be significant, and I have tried solely to shed light on the mystery of one character by means of placing him in context with other inescapable features of *Drood*. This is a detective novel that is far richer in texture than many another, and perhaps that richness makes for its setting forth treasures of varied sorts.

THE LINE-UP
By Walter Albert

The Adventuresses of Sherlock Holmes

Newsletter of B.S.I. scion society. For subscriptions write Mary Ellen Cochon, 52 West 56th Street, New York, NY 10019. I do not subscribe to any of the Doyle-related publications and my information about them is, at best, second-hand. I would welcome corrections of or additions to any of the material in this listing with the information in the items designated "not seen" or "not seen recently" the most urgently in need of confirmation.

The Armchair Detective

Edited by Allen J. Hubin. Published by The Mysterious Press, 129 West 56th Street, New York, NY 10019. Quarterly, $16 per year. Articles, interviews, bibliographies and checklists, reviews, and letters. The oldest continuously publishing critical journal in the field and, in spite of intermittent complaints from fans and charter members about what they see as an increasing emphasis on academic material and a loss of intimacy, the most substantial and most important. Hubin will probably step down as editor at the end of this year (1980), and the announcement of his successor is already being anticipated by the operation of a hyperactive rumor-mill.

The Baker Street Journal

Published quarterly at $10 a year by Fordham University Press, Box L, Bronx, NY 10458. The contents are abstracted and indexed in *Abstracts of English Studies,* copies of which (unlike most of the other magazines in this listing) should be available in any reasonably outfitted college library reference room.

Baker Street Miscellanea

Published quarterly at $5 a year by The Sciolist Press, P.O. Box 2579, Chicago, IL 60690. Hubin described issue 19 of BSM in a recent issue of TAD as "the most polished of Sherlockian publications [with] articles, news and reviews, as well as the latest installment of the useful 'Sherlock Holmes Reference Guide.'" (TAD 13:1, p. 30) Not seen.

Cloak and Dagger

Edited and published by Jim Huang, 66 N. Virginia Ct., Englewood Cliffs, NJ 07362. I have received a notice that this newsletter is resuming publication after a year-long hiatus and Huang invites both contributions and subscriptions. Price is $2 for five monthly issues.

Clues: A Journal of Detection

Semi-annual, $10 for 2 issues. Popular Culture Center, Bowling Green State University, Bowling Green, OH 43403. Another journal by those academic folk who bring us the *Journal of Popular Culture*. The first issue is devoted to studies of the work of John D. MacDonald, with an introduction and appraisal of each piece by JDM. Not seen, but the flyer I received spoke of the first issue in the past tense, leading me to suspect that it is somewhere between conception and distribution.

Collecting Paperbacks?

Bi-monthly, $16 for 6 issues. Lance Casebeer, 934 S.E. 15th, Portland, OR 97214. An informal but useful collection of columns, letters, and notes of pbs, and an advertiser.

Current Crime

Quarterly, 50p. an issue. A British newsletter. For subscriptions write to CC, Box 18, Bognor Regis, Sussex, PQ22 7AA, United Kingdom. Not seen. [*Consists almost entirely of short one- and two-sentence reviews of books published in Great Britain. Worth every new pence of the price. GMT.*]

DAPA-EM

The aging but still lively detective amateur press association publishes a bi-monthly collection of fanzines by members which, most recently, has been appearing in three-volume mailings to accommodate the garrulous, sometimes querulous productions of the 35 members. Subscriptions are not available, but there is a waiting list for prospective members. Information may be obtained from Art Scott, 10365 Wunderlich Drive, Cupertino, CA 95014

DAST Magazine

(Detectives-Agents-Science Fiction-Thriller.) Mostly in Swedish but with some material in English. For information, write (in Swedish or English) to editor Iwan Hedman, Flodins väg 5, S-15200, Strängnäs, Sweden. Not seen recently.

Enigmatika

Quarterly, 40 francs a year. Editor: Jacques Baudou, 4, Rue de l'Avenir, Les Mesneux 51500, Rilly-la-Montagne, France. All the contents are in French, but the articles, bibliographies, filmographies, indexes and checklists provide information on French material not available anywhere else.

The Gazette

Journal of the Rex Stout society, The Wolfe Pack. For membership and journal subscriptions write The Wolfe Pack, P.O. Box 822, Ansonia Station, New York, NY 10023. [*Good luck--I've been trying for six months to get Larry Brooks, who edits this thing, to tell me how much I have to pay him for a subscription and back issues. Still not a peep out of him.*]

The GMS Informant

Edited and published by Don Miller, 12315 Judson Road, Wheaton, MD 20906. News and reviews of SF, fantasy, mysteries, westerns and boardgaming. Published irregularly and no issues seen in 1980. Miller also publishes *The Mystery Nook*, although not recently. He publishes in spurts--as his health permits-- and I would expect to hear from him again before the end of the year. [*That may not happen--Don's health has been very bad lately.*]

Megavore

Bi-monthly, $12 for 6 issues. Edited and published by Grant Thiessen, Pandora's Books Ltd., Box 86, Neche, ND 58265. When *Xenophile* (see below) began to publish irregularly, Weirdbook Press put out two issues of an advertiser (*Fantasy Mongers*) and then joined with the *Unicorn* (Cook-McDowell Publications) to produce *Age of the Unicorn*. Early this year, Cook-McDowell sold their advertiser to Thiessen who has been publishing a fine bibliographical journal (*The Science-Fiction Collector*) for several years. The first issue of the newly-titled journal appeared in June and included articles and checklists along with advertisements of books and magazines for sale.

The John D. MacDonald Bibliophile

Edited by Ed Hirshberg, Department of English, University of South Florida, Tampa, FL 33620. $3 for 2 issues. Continuation of the newsletter/fanzine originally published by Len and June Moffatt.

Mystery

Bi-monthly, $10 for 6 issues. P.O. Box 26251, Los Angeles, CA 90026. A struggling slick of general interest to the mystery fan. Material thin but the intentions are good.

The Not So Private Eye

Edited and published by Andy Jaysnovitch, 6 Dana Estates, Parlin, NJ 08859. The P.I. in film, TV and fiction. Andy J. is one of the most fluent writers in mystery fandom and his TNSPE is essential for the reader of p.i./hardboiled fiction. There is even an unsubstantiated rumor that America's leading LOL scholar is a closet subscriber.

Paperback Quarterly

Edited by Billy C. Lee, 1710 Vincent Street, Brownwood, TX 76801, at $6 for 4 issues. Historical and bibliographical articles and notes on pb publishing. Also letters and columns with the irrepressible Bill Crider as an often-featured contributor. A professional job on all counts.

The Poisoned Pen

Edited and published by Jeffrey Meyerson, 50 First Place, Brooklyn, NY 11231, at $8 for 6 issues. Articles, checklists, reviews and letters. In a fannish world where deadlines are made to be broken, you can almost confirm the accuracy of your calendar by the bi-monthly arrival of TPP.

Polar

Annual subscription for this monthly is 150 francs. Write to Polar, 33 Passage Jouffroy, 75008 Paris, France. A digest-sized, slick mystery magazine of general interest. Films, books, reviews, interviews, letters. The model of what *Mystery* could be. All in French, of course, but there are lots of stills and photos.

The Rohmer Review

Edited and published by Robert E. Briney, 4 Forest Ave., Salem, MA 01970. Editor Briney's elegant fanzine last appeared in 1977. I miss TRR and my only consolation is that Bob is now a DAPA-EM member and his contribution, *Contact Is Not a Verb*, is as absorbing as TRR.

The Thorndyke File

Published by Philip T. Asdell, R.R. #1, Box 355, Frederick, MD 21701. Semi-annual. Not seen.

Xenophile

Edited and published by Nils Hardin, 26 Chapala, #5, Santa Barbara, CA 93101. Irregular publication. $10 per year (bulk rate). "An advertiser and journal devoted to fantastic and imaginative literature." X readers have had to content themselves with meager rations of late. The publication schedule has discouraged advertisers and without ads, Hardin can't publish the other features which made this journal indispensable to the pulp collector, fan and scholar. In spite of Hardin's optimism, X's future does not look promising. I hope that I am wrong about this grim prediction.

I REMEMBER.... B-MOVIES

By Jeff Banks

The very best thing about being a kid (from the kid's point of view) in the Forties was the movies. And I don't mean the "A" pictures either, with their lavish color and super casts. Oft as not parents wanted to see them, and those family outings were find in their way too. But they weren't half the fun of being sent off alone, a dime in one hand (the OPA kept my movie admissions frozen at 9¢ through 1946--and I cried, along with most of my contemporaries, when the price rose to 11¢) and a nickle in the other (for popcorn or candy) to see a pair of satisfying features, a 2-reel comedy, an animated cartoon, and a really thrilling serial chapter.

Now I want to be completely honest and admit that detective films of the era were not my favorites. And with four movie houses, each with program changes twice-a-week besides the Friday and Saturday double feature, I could and did usually find a Western program. (Roy Rogers is currently hosting a syndicated TV rerun of Cowboy B-Movies, but that is beside the point here.) Just counting the four years of World War II, I must have seen more than 3,000 feature movies (towards the end, I spent Saturdays from lunch--which we called "dinner"--"in town" taking in two double features). Even allowing half that total to be westerns, and close to half the rest horror films, I saw most of the detective and mystery movies made between 1935 and 1945. That is what I am going to reminisce about this time.

SERIALS FOR DESSERT

(We are beginning with dessert because that's the way any kid would want his meal.)

Looking back from about a 30 year vantage point, the serials I saw are most vivid in my memory. They were designed to keep the moviegoer coming back for more, even if he didn't particularly want to see the feature(s). How well they did that for others I really don't know, but I am certain they worked like a charm on me. Of those four theaters in my hometown, one showed only Westerns on weekends; one showed mostly Westerns, but with a sprinkling of Horror and Detection; one divided as nearly as possible between those three types; and one had a mixture, but with Mystery-Detection as the main ingredient. Whenever I went to the latter it was usually because of the serial, but I invariably enjoyed most of the rest of the program.

Among the serials, the Batmans, Vigilante, and Capt. America were the ones I liked best of all. They "brought to life" some of my favorite comicbook heroes. Kirk Allyn's Superman serials worked less well for me at the time, though I found them delightful about a decade later when an independent TV station ran them opposite the George Reeves TV Superman. And oddly, when Capt. America was rerun by an independent station a couple of years ago, I cared for it not at all. (Shh! People might think my taste has begun to mature.)

I also enjoyed most of the Ralph Byrd Dick Tracys, and I

certainly liked serials like *Radio Patrol*, *Flying G-Men* and *Nick Carter, Detective*. They weren't my favorites, but I do still remember isolated scenes from them so they must have impressed me more than a little.

I did not see Victor Jory and The Shadow serial--though I could not have been kept away if it had shown in my town. More later on Vic, who may well have been too good an actor for the serials anyway. I did see the serial version of the Hammett-created comicstrip Secret Agent X-9; at least I saw most of it. Measles (or was it mumps?) blasted a two-week hole in the middle that I still regret. Almost as good a spy story was Kane Richmond in *Spy Smasher*. I never saw the feature that was fashioned from the chapter-play, but that I don't regret because the serial was superb. I liked him even better in another that had boxers and girl reporters, but darned if I know at this late date whether it was *Brenda Star--Reporter* or *12 Leather Pushers*.

What was your favorite Mystery serial?

VAS YOU DERE FOR CHARLIE?

Charlie Chan was surely my least favorite Detective movie serials, though I'm sure I saw well over half the 46 feature films. The romantic leads (Kane Richmond in *Charlie Chan in Rio* and *Charlie Chan in Panama*, and Robert Lowery in *Charlie Chan in Reno*, both of whom were already favorites of mine, for instance) were the only redeeming features of the series for me. Certainly, I should mention Ray Milland in *Charlie Chan in London*, too, but if I'm to continue my policy of strict honesty I will admit not even knowing he had been in a Chan film until by chance passing through the room where one of my children was watching this particular movie on TV just a few years ago and catching sight of Milland on the screen.

The Chan movies being the first serials that I remember regular success in beating the detective to most mystery solutions might seem to be something that should raise the series in my individual ratings. Far from it, I see this now as one of the chief reasons I usually do not like the classic type of detective fiction--Christie, Stout, Lathen and other exceptions to this rather firm general rule have been mentioned in other things I've written.

The monotony of the Chan movies--even the "humorous parts" --was what impressed me most about the series. That is what drove me, I believe, to thinking through the generally shallow "mystery". But it was the too-Occidental look of the latter heroes that finally made the whole thing unbearable. By the time Roland Winters, he of the long, slender nose, took over the part, I had seen enough war movies to be sure that he didn't look the least Chinese.

THE SUPER SERIES, AS I SAW THEM

Because of the constant switching of stars I was never able to regard the Philip Marlowe movies as a series, though I find I remember several of the individual films (see below) with great affection. Also, the reader should keep in mind that the six Thin Man movies, which will be discussed under another heading, were (and are) my favorite detective series. Aside from these, several others gave many hours of delight to my childhood.

First, and foremost, the Mike Shayne filsm. In later years I learned that the original group, starring Lloyd Nolan, drew their stories from novels by Chandler and Biggers as often as from Halliday (Dresser). This rather typical Hollywoodian dishonesty has damned the Nolan Shaynes in the eyes of many a mystery fan. And that, says I, is a damned shame, for Noland was a damned fine Shayne--or a fine damned shamus. The thing that bothered me about this series was Nolan's constant switching between the hero and heavy roles in his non-series filmes--he was the original Dr. Kildaire villain (even before Lew Ayres became Kildaire), for instance. My all-time favorite Nolan role, though, he did in his sixties: he was Art Rickerby, a highly placed FBI man in *The Girl Hunters*. That was far the best Mike Hammer movie, due in no small part to Nolan's professionalism.

When Hugh Beaumont took over the Shayne role in the mid-Forties, I felt that the series went rapidly downhill. It may be unfair to blame this on Beaumont, who I perceived later as at least a competent comedic actor; it may be that Nolan simply wisely got out when he felt that the Shayne movies were running out of steam.

I liked George Sanders better as the Falcon than as the Saint, and when Tom Conway took the series over (in *The Falcon's Brother*) I did not like it as much. But I saw and liked them all, and years later when they came on TV, I still did not feel that Conway's acting the role (which I could see by that time was not a demanding one) was significantly inferior to his brother's.

On first sight, I liked the "updated" dozen Sherlock Holmes Rathbone and Bruce movies better than the two "period" ones which had introduced the series. However, having seen all 14 again during the excitement stirred by Meyer's first Holmes book, I find that my judgment on them has reversed itself so that I am now in harmony with majority thought on this series. The topicality of the later group was a definite plus (at least for young moviegoers like myself) when they were first released, but it dates them badly now.

On the other hand, I still do not feel these movies are quite as inverior as I have seen several others comment since my discovery of mystery fandom. Also, the cumulative effect of them helped establish the Rathbone and Bruce team's radio show in the hearts of a huge radio audience, and the feedback from radio listenting helped to make Rathbone the definitive film Holmes.

Boston Blackie was a series I particularly liked. It was also a successful pioneer in making the transition from the big screen to TV. In retrospect, I realize that this success was due in large part to the very cheapness of the movie series; even with the miniscule budgets available in early TV, few production values were lost in the switchover simply because there was not much to be lost. The convincingly tough underworld milieu (the thing I liked best about the series) survived because in those days it didn't cost much to create a setting that looked poor.

THE BIG THREE

I saw and was tremendously impressed by *The Maltese Falcon* (the 1941 version), *Murder, My Sweet* (my favorite Philip Marlowe movie--at least until Mitchum's *Farewell, My Lovely*--a good example of how expensive it has gotten to look poor; and yes, I think I saw them all, including Bogart's which I rate among my "top 10"), and *The Thin Man* (and all five sequels). In the Forties, the latter movie was my favorite detective film, but now that I am in my own forties I ascribe that favoritism mainly to the cumulative effect of the sequels with the same stars continuing to play the Charleses as though born to their roles. Now, I am certain that *The Maltese Falcon* was best, and I have seen both it and *The Thin Man* (and most of the sequels) each of the last four years to give a pretty firm basis to my reassessment. I have not been able to see *Murder, My Sweet* since my days of childhood infatuation with it, but I do have a tape recording of the Lux Radio Theater's version (and have one of *The Thin Man* from the same series, but only a half-hour bowdlerization of *The Maltese Falcon*) which I listen to often, and always with delight.

SLEEPERS

Among the unheralded B-movies I have my personal favorites, as I'm sure do most other older readers of this publication. *D.O.A.** (the asterisk was to lead us to the explanation that the title meant "dead on arrival") is one of them. I have since seen it on TV and not been disappointed, something that can be said of precious few of the movies I enjoyed as a youngster.

Another is *The Crimson Canary*, in which Noah Beery, Jr. (yes, Rockford's dad), was the clever police detective. Did you know that Beery is only 12 years older than "son" James Garner? And, while we're on the subject of *The Rockford Files*, my all-time favorite in the series is the one in which Rocky (a retired trucker) goes unknowingly into partnership in a diner with a retired Mafia leader. The both of them are then hounded relentlessly by a retired FBI man, living in poverty and dining on dogfood in order to be able to carry on his investigation and personal vendetta. This latter retiree's mission is finally completed with Rockford's unwilling assistance. The FBI man's role is unforgettably played by Victory Jory.

I always enjoyed Warren William, whether he was playing Perry Mason (though I later came to prefer the Raymond Burr interpretation), the Lone Wolf (I still think he was the best of several in that part), or Philo Vance (the only one of them I liked, though I don't remember ever seeing Ronald Colman as Vance, and some older fans assure me Colman was best). I's sorry indeed that I didn't see William in the spoof version of *The Maltese Falcon* (*Satan Met a Lady*) for I always felt he delivered his infrequent laugh lines well in the movies I did see. My favorite (at least the best remembered) of his films was *The Lone Wolf Takes a Chance*. I would be interested in reading an article or two on what others consider sadly underrated detective films.

COMEDY RELIEF

   Comedy mysteries are a film genre that I have come to like more as an adult than I did as a kid. I have loved the various Don Westlake movies, and the comparatively recent *The Black Bird* belongs in my "top 10" or awfully close to it. Even the real losers such as *Foul Play* and the Pink Panther series (which has definitely been going on too long to suit me) have their memorable moments.
   Even as a child I delighted in *The Bank Dick* and the Three Stooges crime-detective movies. What I probably should admit is that I loved all the movies (including the 2-reelers) that the Stooges and Fields made, and that now I find that I like most those of their films which include detective elements.

OLD TIME RADIO LIVES

"SAINTS PRESERVE US, MR. KEEN!"

By Carl Larsen

If there are any heavens, let part of mine be a night in the late 1940s. In a small room I will be reluctantly doing homework, perhaps memorizing the capitals of all 48 states. Downstairs my father will be listening to the family radio, a large Zenith. If it is tuned to a news commentator, my father will be talking back to him, using language of which neither the FCC nor my mother approves. If it is tuned to a comedy, say *Amos 'n Andy* or *Charlie McCarthy*, my father will be laughing, at a volume of which my mother does not approve. She will probably be ironing white shirts and blouses for tomorrow. My sisters and brother will be at various stages en route to sleep.

In the small room there is a small white radio, nine inches tall. To this day, it serves as a standard of measurement, summoned up in memory to provide a picture of how much space nine inches occupies. Now, halfway through the alphabetical list of the states, almost perfect at matching capitals and states, I turn it on to reward my scholarship. Not too loudly: study and radio are not a blend of which either my mother or father approves.

It's a Thursday night, how about a half-hour of mystery with *Mr. Keen, Tracer of Lost Persons*? The kindly old investigator, his dull-witted partner, Mike Clancy, and his agitated clients--like many who remember old-time radio, I recall their existence, but not their essence. Happily, the magic of recording has preserved a few examples, of which I have one: "The Bride and Groom Murder Case." My version is truncated, no credits nor commercials. Again happily, reference books exist to fill in details which memory or even complete broadcasts cannot supply.

The program's theme music, believe it or not, was "Someday I'll Find You." Then,

> Our scene opens in a roof garden restaurant which is located atop a fourteen-story building in mid-Manhattan. The floor is crowded with gay people, while at a small table in the corner a young man and his lovely young bride gaze out of the large window at the breath-taking skyline which is New York after dark-- a skyline that is soon destined to become a backdrop for horror.

The young honeymooners, Roy and Olivia, venture out on the terrace to drink in the signts. "Happy darling?... Oh, Great Scott, I forgot to phone my mother!" Olivia is left to finish her moonlight cocktail alone. She finds out that the honeymoon is over: she is hurled off the terrace to her death.

Mr. Keen and Mike Clancy get the case the next day. Mr. Keen speaks straight from his kindly old shoulder: "You mustn't let this tragedy ruin your own life, Roy. You're young, you've got to learn to live with your sorrow." He and Mike (Saints preserve us, Mr. Keen!) proceed to interview the suspects. These include, beside Roy, his mother who faints opportunely, like Lady Macbeth (as you might suspect from that honeymoon phone call, she deserves at least a monograph by S. Freud); the half-brother who did not inherit his fair share; and the half-brother's wife, who gave up a Hollywood career for love. The chief clue is a ring absent-mindedly left on the terrace by the murderer. Trapped by Mr. Keen ("All right, Mike, you can put on the handcuffs"), the culprit dies by defenestration.

"Sure, and that's justice for ya!"

"Yes, Mike, _____ _____ met the same fate ___ dealt ___ victim."* The case is closed.

Bennett Kilpack was Mr. Keen; Jim Kelly played Mike Clancy. The show was produced by Frank and Anne Hummert, well-known for their veritable factory of soap-operas such as *The Romance of Helen Trent*. Starting as a thrice weekly fifteen-minute serial in 1937, *Mr. Keen* became a weekly half-hour in 1943. Sponsors included Bisodol, Kolynos, and Chesterfield. Kolynos is the one I remember; keep your Aims and your Crests; give me a tooth powder with a name like a Greek island!

Mr. Keen's name had a comic-strip obviousness, like Dick Tracy (detective who traces) or Sam Spade, which suggested immediately that subtlety was not going to predominate in the ensuing festivities. This obviousness, carried over into plot, characterization, and dialogue, gave such a show potential appeal to a broad spectrum of the population, encompassing all ages and all degrees of intellectual development. Of course, such programs were easily parodied--who can forget Bob and Ray's *Mr. Trace--Keener Than Most Persons* or Fred Allen's Sam Shovel? But Mike Clancy, forever befuddled by life, was almost beyond parody. Another in the long line of satellite sidekicks stretching back through Tonto, Pancho, Bunny, and Dr. Watson to Sancho Panza, Clancy could be considered a milder-mannered cousin of reporter Michael Axford on *The Green Hornet*. (That's Har-nut, son.)

Being Celts, both Axford and Clancy were permitted to have emotional reactions without the accompanying stigma of weakness or derangement. Additionally, having accents, they made it easier for the audience to sort out the characters on a fast-paced radio show. Being dense, they required constant explanations and reminders which helped the audience to follow the plot while not directly insulting its intelligence. This last consideration also helps to explain all those conversations with dogs and horses which abounded on radio.

On the basis of the example of "The Bride and Groom Murder Case" alone, it is plain that *Mr. Keen* tried to provide entertainment with a moral lesson or two thrown in for good measure. Unchecked greed or jealousy leads directly to tragedy, we must bear up under adversity, criminals are caught and punished, there is justice built into the very fabric of life--all four lessons are underscored by the story. Although much of today's audience might not care for such obvious moralizing (contrast the popularity of the despicable J.R. on *Dallas*, for example), such a combination was evidently quite acceptable in the past: *Mr. Keen* lasted for seventeen years.

Mr. Keen, Tracer of Lost Persons, one of the few radio detectives who had no previous existence in books or films, was a part of radio's golden age. Like it, he has almost vanished,

---

*Names and pronouns have been omitted to protect the curious. No endings or boxtops will be given away during this series.

but not without a trace!
    Could one study successfully while listening to radio?
Saints preserve us, just ask me for a state capital?

SPY SERIES CHARACTERS IN HARDBACK, IV
By Barry Van Tilburg

DOSSIER #24: Commander Esmond Shaw.
CREATED BY: Philip McCutchan
OCCUPATION: Started in the series by working for Naval Intelligence; later turned to working for the super elite 6D2.
ASSOCIATES: Capt. Carberry and Mr. Latimer, his bosses at Naval Intelligence; Max, his boss at 6D2.
WEAPONS: Shaw will use anything possible.
OTHER COMMENTS: Shaw has a bad stomach which keeps him awake at night, due no doubt to the things he has to do. He is a simple, realistic, and believable character, though the later books take on a science fiction quality which make the plots less realistic. My favorite Shaw book is *Hartinger's Mouse*, in which a laboratory mouse used in bacteriological warfare experiments is stolen. This mouse is a carrier of a strain of deadly bacteria. People start to die, but there is a pattern, a human pattern, to the whole thing, and Shaw is sent to find out who, why, and where.

Gibraltar Road (Harrap, 1960).
Redcap (Harrap, 1961).
Warmaster (Harrap, 1963; John Day, 1965).
The Man from Moscow (Harrap, 1963; John Day, 1965).
Bluebolt One (Harrap, 1964).
Moscow Coach (Harrap, 1965; John Day, 1966).
The Dead Line (Harrap, 1966).
Skyprobe (Harrap, 1966; John Day, 1967).
The Screaming Dead Balloons (Harrap, 1968; John Day, 1968).
The Bright Red Businessman (Harrap, 1969; John Day, 1969).
Hartinger's Mouse (Harrap, 1970).
This Drakotny... (Harrap, 1971).
Sunstrike (Hodder, 1979).
Corpse (Hodder, 1980).

DOSSIER #25: Simon Shard.
CREATED BY: Philip McCutchan.
OCCUPATION: Chief Inspector of Scotland Yard, seconded to British Security.
ASSOCIATES: Hedge, his boss, whom he really doesn't care for; Harry Kenwood, his assistant; Beth, his wife.
WEAPONS: Service revolvers.
OTHER COMMENTS: Shard, like Shaw, is a very realistic character. He always worries about his wife and his job, and he allows his mother-in-law to meddle in his life. But he can be hard as nails when the occasion calls for it; in *The Eros Affair* he even threatens to blackmail his boss to get some answers.

Call for Simon Shard (Harrap, 1974).
A Very Big Bang (Harrap, 1975).
Blood Run East (Hodder, 1976).
The Eros Affair (Hodder, 1977).
Blackmail North (Hodder, 1978).

DOSSIER #26: Talos Cord.
CREATED BY: Robert MacLeod (Bill Knox).
OCCUPATION: Agent for United Nations Security.
ASSOCIATES: Andrew Beck, his boss.
WEAPONS: Neuhausen 9mm. automatic pistol.
OTHER COMMENTS: Referred to as a Peacemaker, Cord controls or or deals with attacks on Free World policy as they are planned or executed.
Cave of Bats (John Long, 1964; Holt, Rinehart, 1966).
Lake of Fury (John Long, 1966).
Isle of Dragons (John Long, 1967).
Place of Mists (John Long, 1969).
Path of Ghosts (John Long, 1971; McCall, 1971).
Nest of Vultures (John Long, 1973).

DOSSIER #27: Bulldog Drummond.
CREATED BY: Sapper (M.C. McNeile, continued by Gerard Fairlie).
OCCUPATION: Starts as adventurer and later works for Military Intelligence.
ASSOCIATES: McIver, a policeman with whom he occasionally works.
WEAPONS: Pistols.
OTHER COMMENTS: Drummond started the series as head of a vigilante force called "The Black Gang". The first four books deal with his fight with arch-criminal Carl Peterson. Later, during the war years, Drummond gets put into intelligence work. Like Gordon Ashe's Patrick Dawlish, Drummond is a big man; he makes others feel like dwarfs, and he uses his physical powers as well as his mental powers. George Sanders played Drummond in the movies.
Bulldog Drummond (Doran, 1921; Hodder, 1921).
The Black Gang (Doran, 1922; Hodder, 1922).
The Third Round (Doubleday, 1924; Hodder, 1924).
The Final Count (Hodder, 1926).
The Female of the Species (Doubleday, 1928).
Temple Tower (Doubleday, 1929; Hodder, 1929).
Bulldog Drummond Strikes Back (Doubleday, 1933; published as *Knockout* by Hodder, 1934).
The Return of Bulldog Drummond (Hodder, 1934; published as *Bulldog Drummond Returns* by Doubleday, 1935).
Bulldog Drummond at Bay (Doubleday, 1935; Hodder, 1935).
The Challenge (Doubleday, 1937; Hodder, 1937).
Bulldog Drummond on Dartmoor (Hodder, 1939); Hillman-Curl, 1939).
Bulldog Drummond Attacks (Hodder, 1939; Gateway, 1940).
Captain Bulldog Drummond (Hodder, 1945; Musson, 1945).
Bulldog Drummond Stands Fast (Hodder, 1947).
Hands Off Bulldog Drummond (Hodder, 1949).
Calling Bulldog Drummond (Hodder, 1951).

DOSSIER #28: Mr. Moto.
CREATED BY: John Phillips Marquand.
OCCUPATION: Agent for Japanese Intelligence.
ASSOCIATES: None known.
WEAPONS: Automatic pistols.
OTHER COMMENTS: Mr. Moto would rather solve problems peacefully, if possible. With the coming of World War II, Marquand changed him from a good guy to a bad guy. In the movies the character was changed from an intelligence agent into a detective; Peter Lorre portrayed Mr. Moto on the screen.

Thank You, Mr. Moto (Little, 1936; Jenkins, 1937).
Think Fast, Mr. Moto (Little, 1936; Hale, 1937).
Mr. Moto Is So Sorry (Little, 1938; Hale, 1939).
Mr. Moto Takes a Hand (Hale, 1940).
Last Laugh, Mr. Moto (Little, 1942; Hale, 1943).
Stopover: Tokyo (Little, 1957; Collins, 1957).

DOSSIER #29: Christopher Bond.
CREATED BY: Wyndham Martyn.
OCCUPATION: Works for British Intelligence.
ASSOCIATES: No regulars.
WEAPONS: Pistols.
OTHER COMMENTS: Bond is an adventurer, always looking for trouble. During the war years the British use his reckless powers to combat the Nazis. In *Capture* Bond is sent in to penetrate Nazi Intelligence, and he learns of a plot to destroy a secret allied airbase.
Christopher Bond--Adventurer (Jenkins, 1932).
Spies of Peace (Jenkins, 1933).
The Denemede Mystery (Jenkins, 1936).
The Marrowby Myth (Jenkins, 1938).
The Noonday Devils (Jenkins, 1939).
Capture (Jenkins, 1940).
Shadow Agent (Jenkins, 1941).
Cairo Crisis (Jenkins, 1945).
The Chromium Cat (Jenkins, 1952).

IT'S ABOUT CRIME
By Marvin Lachman

William McIlvanney's *Laidlaw* was one of the most highly praised mysteries of the late 1970's. Jon Breen, whose opinion I respect, called it "a crime fiction cornerstone." I disagree. McIlvanney can write; his Glasgow setting comes alive. He creates real people, including a titular hero who is heir apparent to Lew Archer and Martin Beck in the guilt sweepstakes. Laidlaw is described thusly:

> He was drinking too much--not for pleasure, just sipping it systematically, like low-proof hemlock. His marriage was a maze nobody had ever mapped, an infinity of habit and hurt and betrayal down which Ena and he wandered separately, meeting occasionally in the children.

Beautiful. But no one can keep up that quality in a long novel, and eventually terminal metamoritis does the story in. Its accomplice is a predictable ending (all along we know the murderer). McIlvanney has a lot he wants to say about crime and the responsibility we all bear for those who commit it. What he says may be valid, but his message would have been better borne on the wings of a good story.

An even more disappointing book is Thomas Sanchez's highly praised *Zoot Suit Murders* (1978), just reprinted in paperback. Dealing with murders against a background of the World War II violence between Mexican-American teen-agers and servicemen on leave in Los Angeles, it fails on every count. It is pretentious and yet is neither a good mystery nor a good mainstream novel. Its characters and war-time setting are never believable. Furthermore, it is anachronistic, like those television movies allegedly set in the 30's or 40's in which actors insist on retaining their 1980 long hair styles. In 1942, people neither talked of ballpoint pens nor used expressions like "no way" or "turning tricks."

Mystery writers from Poe to Asimov have written science fiction. I suspect that in addition to having a second market, they recognized that fans of both genres are receptive to good story-telling. I recently found an excellent tale of Woolrich-type suspense, "The Man Who Returned," in Ballantine's paperback collection, *The Best of Edmond Hamilton*. It was originally published in the pulp *Weird Tales* for February 1935.

Those of us who are parents and wish to encourage our children in what we believe to be a harmless addiction have a problem. What do we provide that is age-appropriate and will pave the way for a life-long love of the mystery? Success is problematical. Because my son was a fast reader and had enjoyed Eve Titus' Basil (the mouse detective) of Baker Street I encouraged him to read *A Study in Scarlet* at age nine. He stopped halfway through it and hasn't read a mystery in the last 13 years. No, I haven't disowned him.... Yet.

Assume that my unfortunate experience is atypical. For children about eight to ten I recommend the Encyclopedia Brown stories of Donald J. Sobol. LeRoy Brown, son of Idaville's police chief, promises to solve cases for 25¢ a day, plus expenses. Judging by a sampling of Sobol's most recent short story collection, *Encyclopedia Brown and the Case of the*

Midnight Visitors (Bantam Skylark, $1.50), this is a good beginning. The stories are fast-moving, have a touch of humor, and, most important of all, use real (albeit simple) deduction to solve crimes. For a slightly older audience, the same publisher has a series of books about "teenage super sleuth" Kay Tracey by Frances K. Judd. After peeking inside *The Double Disguise* and *In the Sunken Garden* ($1.75 each), I'd say these might be about right for ages ten to twelve.

A deliberately Jewish Private Eye is the brainstorm of Leo Rosten in *Silky!* (1979), just reprinted by Bantam. The only other Jewish detective I can think of, except for Rabbi Small, is Simon's Moses Wine, but he is too anti-Establishment to admit his roots. Rumor has it that Chandler, who had at various times called his detective Mallory, Malvern, Dalmus, Carmady, and Evans, was considering Philip Marmelstein. He was persuaded to change his character's name to Philip Marlowe and NOT title his first novel *The Big Shlep*. The rest is history. There is also a rumor that Patricia Wentworth's Maud Silver is Jewish. A yenta she may be, but Jewish? I doubt it.

However, Rosten's Sidney "Silky" Pincus is Jewish, and the book requires a 14 page glossary to translate the dozens of Yiddish expressions italicized on almost every page. Rosten's definitions are very amusing, as befits the author of *The Education of H*Y*M*A*N K*A*P*L*A*N* and *Treasury of Jewish Quotations*. The detection is primitive, though Silky operates a detective agency cleverly called "Watson and Holmes, Inc." The book is lively and amusing, and I especially enjoyed the climax in Lincoln Center, to which the author delivers a well-deserved paean.

> The word "normal" could be applied to neither his brain nor to his body.... During his active days his powerful frame had carried him successfully through many an ugly situation. Now that his work was necessarily of a sedentary character, the great muscles had largely turned to fat and his figure had become enormous.... He leant back in his chair for some time, his eyes closed....

A description of Nero Wolfe? No, it is Supt. Fraser in Henry Wade's first book, *The Verdict of You All* (1926). Not Wade's best, it is nonetheless fast reading like many Golden Age books. That is because it contains no unnecessary descriptions or Freudian overtones. The characters are distinct, albeit cardboard. The story and the puzzle are sufficient to carry the day.

Verdict is ostensibly serious, except for a butler whose misuses of such French expressions as "decolletage" and "couchez bien" is amusing. Still, I wonder at Wade's seriousness in naming characters. We have Sir Horace Stille; Mr. Deeping Waters; Sir Edward Floodgate; Daniel Flush; Mr. Suckling; Sir Isaac Sharpe; William Goke, office boy for Petitt & Fogg, solicitors; the firm of Buckett & Buckett, billbrokers; Hector Stentorius; Mr. Crabbitt. Shades of Dickens!

It is always interesting to discover a series character for an author we were sure never created one. Frank "Rosie" Rosenfeld, a U.S. Intelligence agent whose cover is as refrigerator salesman, appears in Helen MacInnes' *Venetian Affair* (1963) and *The Double Image* (1966). The latter book is dedicated to our Cold Warriors whom she dubs "the Veterans of

Foreign Peace." Always anti-Nazi and anti-Soviet, MacInnes hits upon a perfect scheme in *Image*. She has as villain a Communist who infiltrated the Nazis in World War II, planning for a post-war takeover by killing democrats. Like most of MacInnes it is dreadfully padded, using 300 pages to tell what Michael Gilbert does better in under 30.

Two recent books comprise one of the smallest sub-genres of the mystery, namely books in which the Academy Award statuette ("Oscar") is the murder weapon. One book, still unread, is Thomas Gifford's *Hollywood Gothic* (1979). The other, unfortunately read, is Zebra's paperback original, *You'll Die Tonight* (1979) by Marjorie J. Grove. This is a terrible book with phony topical references, the most outrageous brand-name dropping this side of Ian Fleming, and a cliché-ridden ending. The character's names are either silly)"Pamela Tooth" and "Miss Van Ginkle") or confusing (two are named "Marcella" and "Marcello"). It is not funny enough to be a spoof, nor serious enough to be a decent mystery. So far, Norma Schier is the only Zebra author who has earned her stripes.

MYSTERY*FILE

Short Reviews by Steve Lewis

John M. Reilly, ed. *Twentieth Century Crime and Mystery Writers.* St. Martin's Press, 1980, 1568 pp., $50.00.

    For the hardcore fan of mystery fiction, there are two absolutely indispensable reference works. *The Bibliography of Crime Fiction, 1749-1975* by Allen J. Hubin (Publisher's Inc., 1979) is a gigantic, comprehensive listing by author of all the mystery/detective/suspense fiction ever published. Whatever gaps in important information that volume left behind have now been filled, and more than admirably, by this mammoth compendium of crime, the second volume in St. Martin's ongoing series produced under the overall title of Twentieth Century Writers of the English Language.
    This book contains biographies and bibliographies of over 600 authors of detective fiction. For the most part each is complete enough to satisfy both the cursory reader and the dedicated fan. Many of the writers themselves include a short commentary on their work or on the field in general. And as if this were not enough, closing out each entry is a signed critical essay that attempts to summarize each writer's career and to place his or her output into an overall perspective.
    These essays, written by other authors, learned college scholars, or just plain fans (sometimes all three in just one person), are both the highlight of the book and at the same time the source of the greatest produced frustration. Each essayist does his best to make sure his favorite writers do not get overlooked. Admittedly, not all authors are of the first rank, but how can there be so many writers at the top of the second rank?
    The frustration comes because there are just too many books and the clamor for the need to read them all is just too loud. Not in one lifetime could any one person hope to make more than a dent in the accumulation of books covered here.
    Top honors for productivity must go to John Creasey, whose list of published crime fiction covers 13 pages. (He also wrote Westerns and romances, and it takes another three pages to list those, 560 or so books in all.) In contrast, there are writers like William Brittain and James Holding who are included even though they have not yet published a single book between them (albeit hundreds of short stories), John Gregory Dunne is here, even though he has published only one work of crime fiction in total, the brilliant recent tour de force, *True Confessions*.
    The bibliographies probably constitute the weakest link in what this book attempts to do. Besides the prolific writers for the American pulp magazines of the 20s, 30s and 40s, many of whom are included here, there is a British writer named Herbert Harris who has published something like 3,000 short stories. Only a selection of these are given, and thankfully so.
    Some famous science fiction writers like Isaac Asimov and Ray Bradbury seem to have crept in, suggesting that whatever fences there are between the two fields are not strong enough to keep a good writer categorized.

Christie, Doyle, Hammett, Chandler, all the big names of crime fiction are here, of course. Of the ones omitted, the most worthy of possible inclusion are John Evans and Kathleen Moore Knight. If these two seem to have slipped your memory, it's still the best way I know of to suggest how complete this magnificient volume is.

In spite of the price tag, no mystery fan is going to want to be without this book--and I guarantee that it won't just sit on the shelf. (This review, and subsequent reviews marked with an asterisk, have appeared earlier in the Hartford *Courant*.)

A.E.W. Mason. *Murder at the Villa Rosa*. Scribner's Crime Classics, 1979, 216 pp., $2.25. Originally published in 1909.

A classic? Consider the copyright date and the fact that here it is, in print again. How many good books can you think of that you can't say that about? And how many people of good judgment must have read this book by now? If it's a classic, it will have had to have earned the title.

It is dated. If it were to be submitted to a publisher as newly written, there's no doubt a revision would be demanded. Reading the first chapter relieves some fears, however--the symptoms of old age are there, but the book has not yet succumbed to the afflictions of rigor mortis.

In that first chapter, with precise pictorial writing Mason describes the first meeting of Mr. Ricardo with Mlle. Celie. She is on the verge of melancholy hysteria and despair outside a French Casino; next she is being soothed by the wealthy young English inventor, Mr. Wethermill.

On the very next night Celie's benefactress, whose companion she is, is robbed and murdered. The girl stands accused, at least of complicity. All the evidence, as well as the testimony of the maid, points directly to her. Nor does her background as a stage-variety spiritualist sepak well on her behalf.

Mr. Wethermill asks that the famed M. Hanaud of the Paris Surete be called in. Hanaud is not only a gifted detective, but he is also a forerunner of all those other masterminds who know, or guess, and do not tell. Of course I know that Conan Doyle often allowed Holmes to lapse into this poor excuse for a story-telling mode, but at least Holmes never insulted Watson, at least not directly, nor did he ever ridicule him for poorly asked questions, as Hanaud so badly treats Ricardo.

Speaking of whom--on pages 79-80 of this edition Ricardo very nicely summarizes the eight salient features he sees in the mystery. Included in the challenges Hanaud makes to the questions that Ricardo then asks is one based on one of the very same points that Ricardo has just raised. The latter (as a gentleman?) accepts the rebuke when Hannaud loudly suggests that he has foolishly missed a vital point of the case.

The mystery is solved by page 143. The remainder of the book recounts the vinal version of the reconstructed crime, and Hanaud's feeble attempts to explain the guesses in deduction that he made.

Well, as you can see, I was already biased. This may be too harsh a judgment, and by no account should you take this to mean that Hanaud's version is impossible. It's just that with the facts *as described*, I submit that there is no reader in the world who would have come to the same conclusion as he did, except by guesswork, pure and simple.

A classic? From a historical point of view, perhaps so. As a mystery, it's an outdated one. They just don't write them like this any more. (C minus)

Art Bourgeau. *A Lonely Way to Die*. Charter 49706, 1980, 185 pp., $1.95.

Canada as a locale for a detective story happened to be mentioned in passing a couple of books back. If murderous mayhem is what's on your mind, there are, of course, hundreds of other sites to choose from. Los Angeles and the Big Apple don't have a universal monopoly on the crime. It must just seem that way.

But take Cannibal Springs, Tennessee, for instance. It's located about halfway between Nashville and Chattanooga. I didn't look it up on the map, but even if there is such a place, I'm not so sure than anyone has bothered telling Rand McNally about it.

Snake Kirlin and F.T. Zevich are a couple of good ole boys, just out of the Marines and back in Snake's hometown, looking for the fishing holes and other fine memories of his youth.

An alternative title for this book might have been *The Hardy Boys Get Laid*.

The jokes are crude, pointed, funny, and *old*. According to F.T., as the two heroes prepare to investigate the death of the hairdresser's assistant by rattleless rattlesnake poisoning, "When you eliminate all the shit, whatever you're left with has got to be it."

All devout Sherlock Holmesians, please take note.

My mistake, and don't let it be yours, was in thinking that this was a detective story. Wrong. The clues lead nowhere, the deductions are a waste of time, and the pistons don't work either. It sur was fun to read, and I'll probably read their next adventure, if the fates be so kind, but even tied up in a gunny sack with a typewriter in a dark room, I don't think there's one of us who couldn't have done a better job of working out a real mystery to go will all the good buddy fooferaw. (C minus)

Phillips Lore. *The Looking Glass Murders*. Playboy, 1980, 192 pp., $1.95.

The first Leo Roi detective mystery, *Who Killed the Pie Man?*, was published in hardcover back in 1975 by Saturday Review Press. Nothing further was heard about him until earlier this year when Playboy Press reprinted the book in paperback. It is now fairly obvious that Lore has had a few more Roi stories stored away in a trunk someplace since back then, for two more in the series have suddenly appeared in rapid succession as Playboy paperback originals. (So fast, in fact, that I still haven't seen a copy of what apparently is the second in the series, *Murder Behind Closed Doors*.)

Leo Roi is not a private detective, as he himself will gladly inform you. He is an investigative attorney. But as with Perry Mason, there is very little difference. He is also, excuse the expression, filthy rich. I do not mind this, I am only a little jealous, but the continuing details of his home furnishings, his wardrobe, his fleet of automobiles, these I find boring. You know?

He is married, happily so, and his wife Christina actively helps him with his cases. They are also very lovingly trying to start a family. This is boring too.

The case itself is not without interest. A male middle-aged professor has been living with a student, a coed, also very happily. She is murdered (her name is Alice), and he (his name is Charles Dodo) is accused.

Leo Roi is slick, and the D.A. is dumb. And I hate books in which the culprit is known to everyone but the reader and he is caught by the simple expedient of placing some human bait in a trap.

However, any author who has the theory he has about the reasons behind the decline of American society that Leo Roi expresses for him on pages 44 and 45 should definitely not stay unread. It's just unfortunate that he doesn't write very good mysteries. (C)

Michael Gilbert. *The Killing of Katie Steelstock*. Harper & Row, 1980, 293 pp., $10.95.

As a kind of bonus, we get two stories in one. Katie's death is the obvious reason for the rather dry murder investigation that follows. What we also get, and what fans of legal manipulations and maneuverings like myself will find of much greater interest, is at least a preliminary look at how the defense for the accused goes about making plans for the ensuing trial. Part of their strategy has little to do with the case itself, consisting instead of weighing and working on the personal strengths and idiocyncrasies of the man from Scotland Yard placed in charge of the investigation.

Katie herself was a TV star. After her death, and then only, we discover the two sides there were of her. For the most part, the village folk of Hannington saw her as their fair-headed girl. In London they knew her as an ambitious conniver with little she was unwilling to do to maintain her drive to the top.

This this is a mystery novel with some emphasis on character should be abundantly clear. Even so, the ending is one that may come as something of a surprise. A goodly number of loose ends are left still trailing, and unmitigated coincidence looms large in the overall scheme of things. (B minus)*

Donald Zochert. *Another Weeping Woman*. Rinehart and Winston, 1980, 262 pp., $9.95.

It took longer than it should have, but it finally came to me. What the first few chapters read like is what the old radio program "Pat Novak, for Hire" sounded like. Maybe you remember it. Jack Webb played the title role, a touch, world-weary man-for-all-jobs who keeps finding himself in a peck of trouble, usually of the murder variety.

The narrator of this tale is named Nick Caine, a man whose background is never completely revealed, but that's the kind of man he is, and that's the kind of story he stumbles into.

As you read it, you'll find it mellowing somewhat, into the laid-back, weather-beaten and melancholy mode that has recently epitomized Rocky Mountain mystery fiction. The scenes flicker incessantly back and forth between Denver and the wilderness country of Montana, save for one brief interlude taking place in one of the all-white fortresses that find themselves surrounded by the no-man's-land of urban Chicago.

It all begins with a dead girl, a girl shot dead before a grizzly got to her, a girl dead before the bullet reached her brain. She was looking for her father, but she never found him. Nick Caine picks up the search, and all he finds are memories, a mother's heartbreaks, and murder, a continuing sequence of death by violence. He has been drifting for a year or more before being persuaded into taking the case. He has been out of action for too long, and his reflexes are slow.

And at times the story feels as though it is drifting as well. The ending is overdone, as if intent on stifling itself in a morass of overpowering melodrama. But before then, well, the better hard-boiled detective novel is built on nuances and subtle shades of meaning, not wholly on fast-paced action, and so if that's the sort of literature that catches your attention, most of what goes before should be exactly what you're looking for. (B)*

Richard North Patterson. *The Lasko Tangent*. Ballantine, 1980, 202 pp., $1.95.

Yes, it sounds like a spy thriller, it's packaged like a spy thriller, but what this book precisely is not is--aw, you guessed it. It's not a spy thriller.

What it really is is a novel about the dirty business of laundering money. That is to say, it's a detective story, as told in today's most *au courant* Washingtonian (DC) style.

Lasko is the President's favorite industrialist, but his background has more shade than Forest Lawn--not that anyone has ever proved anything. The President, who is unnamed, but --well, let's just say that only the names have been changed.

Christopher Kenyon Paget is a lawyer for the Prosecution Bureau of the United States Economics Crime Commission. (And I'll wager you didn't even know there was one.) He's young, idealistic, very much a crusader for what he believes in. A chance tip about some possible stock manipulation takes him to Boston, where he watches in horror as his witness, who works for Lasko, is run down by a hit-and-run driver. Higher things are cooking.

This is a cynical novel, and you don't have to dig very far to discover it. According to the inside front cover, Patterson worked for the special prosecutor in the Watergate uncover-up, and his is the voice of authenticity. Paget continually has to fight pressure from higher-ups, without ever knowing who or where the enemy is, and he has a narrow escape or two before he does.

On the other hand, none of this "real Washington" stuff is really nes (here's where I'm being cynical), and it's all wrapped up in the end a little more tightly than real life ever seems to be. (B)

Mike Fredman. *Kisses Leave No Fingerprints.* St. Martin's, 1979, 160 pp., $8.95.

This is a private eye story, but as such, while nothing very much out of the ordinary seems to happen, this is definitely not your ordinary private eye sort of story. A great part of this is unquestionably due to the fact that Willie Halliday is a vegetarian, a non-drinker, and a student of Asiatic religions on the side--not exactly your standard sort of private eye.
Nor does he take on divorce cases as a rule, but he does in this one, and then simply because he finds himself moonstruck in love with the woman who hires him, and thus is easily persuaded. That she cares zip about him is obvious to the reader, but not entirely to Willie, who tells the tale. Not many surprises follow, but even so, Fredman nevertheless seems to have neatly captured a haunting, dreamlike essence of the fictional world-wide brotherhood of knight-errants reincarnated in today's world as private investigatory agents. (C plus)

Nick Carter. *Suicide Seat.* Charter, 1980, 217 pp., $2.25.

Nick Carter, Killmaster, has his hands full this time. He's on the trail of a gang of white slavers who have accidentally made off with the beautiful virgin daughter of a world-powerful OPEC oil sheik. And on Nick Carter's trail is an international gang of terrorists who are apparently intent on wiping out every single agent employed by Carter's secret government organization, AXE.† Now, unfortunately, AXE itself has just been axed, dismantled by some top-level White House worrywarts, and its former director, David Hawk, has disappeared, no one knows where.
Mexico. New York City. Washington, DC. Monte Carlo. Zurich.
Mame Ferguson. Angela Negri. Traudl Heitmyer. Lotus Fong.
By page 111 it was when I really knew I'd had enough. Angie's been kidnapped again, and Nick Carter's been left for dead.
Except.
He isn't dead.
He does have a little bit of a headache, perhaps.
Personally, I think the guy's nuts. Back on page 70, after being briefed rather briefly by Senator Lovett about the missing sheiklette, he abruptly heads for the bathroom and climbs for safety down the outside wall of the hotel. From four floors up.
Why?
Don't ask me.
How the hell would I know? (F)

---

†Offhand, I can't tell you what AXE stands for, but if you'd really like to know, maybe Guy can find out for you.

Michael Z. Lewin. *Outside In*. Knopf, 1980, 216 pp., $8.95.

Most of the work that Lewin has previously produced in the field of detective fiction has been steady if not spectacular private eye fare. Albert Samson, the hero he has used most often, is known as the cheapest detective in Indianapolis, which means that he invariably gets stuck with the cases no one else will take.

None of this, however, adequately paves the way for the tables that Lewin turns upon himself in this, his latest effort. With a nod to the credo always given the beginning writer, "Write what you know," Lewin's newest protagonist is a middle-aged writer named Willie Werth, whose life has grown soft and comfortable from the proceeds gained over the years from a long series of mystery adventures starring that premier private eye, Hank Midwinter.

Now, Hank Midwinter is the kind of guy who outhammers Mickey Spillane's hero, for example, but his author, who finds himself compelled to try to help the police investigate the murder of a friend, quickly discovers that real cops are not like, and do not like, fiction.

Werth is also going through a minor domestic crisis with his wife, who tolerates but who does not always understand the artistic muse. Nor is Werth (nor the reader, for that matter) entirely sure that part of what attracts him so greatly to the case is not the presence at home of his friend's daughter, whose newly found fame is for having made one of "those movies" back in New York.

The combination of Werth's case and the eventual wrapping up of Midwinter's own latest caper is a synergistic entanglement that finds each feeding off the other in alternating chapters. The result is a highly amusing and yet an intensely introspective view of the world of fiction as it exists within its very own shell of reality.

Or perhaps, as Lewin is strongly suggesting, with the right perspective, why couldn't that be taken to read the other way around just as well? (A minus)*

Edwin Leather. *The Duveen Letter*. Doubleday/Crime Club, 1980, 182 pp., $8.95.

The dictionary definition of "serendipity" describes it as the happy quality of finding desirable objects quite by accident. Here, to give an example which stretches the definition only a little bit, but certainly where you might least expect it, in a pair of recently published works of detective fiction, is as fine a double introduction into the parallel worlds of fine arts and antiques as you could find anywhere.

As in most endeavors, involved here are levels of expertise and familiarity that those of us on the lower echelons are only vaguely aware of. It always comes with no little amount of satisfaction, not to mention fascination, whenever we're given the chance like this to pick the brains of even a fictional expert, no matter what field.

Take this book. In it the renown Viennese art dealer Rupert Conway is flown all the way to New York City to assist in authenticating a priceless collection of Renaissance oils. Minute details, such as the artist's technique in painting ears and hands, or the texture of such objects in the background as trees, are said to have exposed more forgeries than any ultra-modern laboratory technician has ever done.

There is another puzzle for Conway to decipher, however, and that is why an apparently genuine painting should come with an entirely phoney letter of authentication. The trail leads him back to Paris, where his diligence is responsible for uncovering yet another of those so many tragic tales still the European legacy of World War II.

Another strand of the plot concerns the attempted defection of an East German SSD officer to the West. On a purely story level, the two halves of the tale run headlong together and are intermeshed only with a noticeably strong dose of coincidence. Too much of the too little action seems also to occur offstage. The urbane Mr. Conway, who has appeared in both of Mr. Leather's previous mysteries, gets his feathers ruffled only just a little this time. (C plus)*

Jonathan Gash. *The Grail Tree*. Harper & Row, 1980, 219 pp., $10.95.

In absolute contrast, there is Lovejoy, of Lovejoy Antiques, Inc., the scruffy hero of sorts of the two previous detective novels written by Jonathan Gash. Here he is again, and somehow still managing to scrape by, both in business, and in his many and varied love affairs.

Lovejoy has, nevertheless, an inborn instinct for the authentic antique--a little bell rings somewhere inside at the merest sniff of one--a handy knack to have, too, since England is apparently awash with myriads of fine imitations being merrily produced every minute of the day by scores of skilled, industrious craftsmen.

In the guise of guiding a young apprentice-assistant named Lydia into the many intricacies of his profession, Lovejoy casually tells us in passing all there is to know, and more certainly than we are ever likely to appreciate, about Sheraton wine tables, Hepplewhite elbow chairs, Regency silverware, and (as the ads would say) much, much more.

Unfortunately, some endless hugger-mugger about some not-so-splendid Satsuma vases slows the tempo down considerably, and keeping track of our hero's motley group of fellow dealers is a requirement that gradually becomes more and more of a chore.

Lovejoy is a character of no great outward appeal, but he knows his business, and his zealous devotion to it is all but enough to make acceptable the rest of his warted personality. It should be noted, however, that it will be strictly those of the male chauvinistic persuasion whom the ending, a mildly happy fantasy of sorts, will please the most. (C)*

Wolf Rilla. *The Chinese Consortium*. Signet, 1980, 251 pp., $2.50.

Despite its extensive Coca-Colonization, the Orient, to Western minds, is still the land of mysterious evil. The sinister leers of Fu Manchu are gone, but they have been replaced by the equally sinister manipulations of chairmen of the boards of companies with names like the innocuous-sounding Eastern International Banking Corporation. If anyone besides the hords of domino-pushing Communists has in mind the conquest and control of the world, it would be the likes of the anonymous employers of the faceless Mr. Wongs.

Candice Freeman is a beautiful lady photographer, on assignment in Bangkok for *Era* magazine. Here she stumbles across one of the tentacles of just such a conglomeration of business interests that know no territorial limits such as the artificial boundaries between countries. And the corner of southeast Asia through which her ensuing investigations take her most certainly is not the Orient of the travel posters.

Wolf Rilla is said to be a film producer. A friend of Candice says on page 131 of her findings to that point, "I mean, it's all a bit like a B movie." Exactly.

The intent, however, is realism, and it's in pursuit of that goal that the book's such a downer. It's not fun to read, as were the adventures of Fu Manchu. The rich are solidly in control now, there is nothing to stay their hand, and there's little offered here to serve as a ray of hope, save for what you may safely glean from the brief afterthought of an epilogue.

If one of the reasons you read detective fiction is because you like problems which have solutions, you will probably not like this book. (C)

John Dickson Carr. *The Door to Doom and Other Detections*. Edited and with an introduction by Douglas G. Greene. Harper & Row, 1980, 352 pp., $12.95.

For this audience it goes without saying that mystery author John Dickson Carr will be remembered longest for his many unmatchable novels of locked-room detection, published both under his name and as the easily identifiable Carter Dickson.

In his work the greatest emphasis was most often on atmosphere--and what better magician's device to thwart the mind and eye of the reader could there be than clouds of (figuratively) black swirling darkness and ominous threats of the supernatural? Such hints rarely extended beyond what was needed to trick the reader's thoughts into taking yet another false trail, however. Carr's conservative roots never allowed him to stray an iota from the credo of fair-play detection he so firmly believed in. To the discerning reader, the clues were always there, but if you missed them you needn't worry-- you were far from being alone!

In his introduction to this anthology of previously uncollected short work, Douglas Greene down-plays Darr's ability at characterization, but I demur. True, as with most of Carr's contemporaries in what is fondly called "The Golden Age of Detection," the story was the thing. I still suspect that few who have read any of the cases solved by Carr's most famous character, Dr. Gideon Fell, will ever forget the picture they have in their minds of that jovial, triple-chinned detective with the shovel hat, bumbling manners, and the razor-sharp mind for the smallest false detail. Carr just did not happen to believe that the personal life of his detective was a matter of concern to his readers.

The stories in this collection are themselves a mixed bag. They range from the early stories of Carr's first detective, Henri Bencolin of the Paris police, recently discovered in the pages of his college's literary magazine, to a selection of radio plays from the famous CBS series "Suspense", vintage early 1940s, to a trio of horror stories done a few years earlier for the pulp magazines. Needless to add, when Carr wrote a horror story, it was a horror story. Nor has Greene included (or, more likely, he could not find) a story, no matter its source, which does not reflect an obvious professional finesse in mixing plot with atmosphere.

Also included are a pair of short Sherlockian playlets, parodies for which perhaps the best one might say for them is that you had to be there. Closing out the book, just before the inclusive 26-page bibliography, is Carr's famous essay on "The Grandest Game in the World," the game he played with his readers for over forty years. The game of fool-him-if-you-can, but never at all costs.

John Dickson Carr died in 1977. After finishing this book, the only regret one can have is that there are no more stories out there somewhere to be discovered someday to make up another such volume as this. There are more radio plays, to be sure, but so low is the state of dramatic radio in this country today, it seems highly unlikely that any publisher would consider a followup collection of more of these to have a chance for commercial success. But we have the novels, and the other stories, don't we, a wealth of riches to read and enjoy, if not for the first time, why then, again and again.

(rating the stories alone, I'd go no higher than a B, but for the whole book, including the introduction and the bibliography, it's a solid A for sure.)*

VERDICTS
(More Reviews)

John Lutz. *Jericho Man*. Morrow, 1980, 250 pp., $10.95.

In his recent novels John Lutz has taken subjects with best-seller, wide-screen potential--a Bigfoot-like monster of the Ozarks in *Bonegrinder*, a Liddy figure out to kill the disgraced ex-president and henchmen in *Lazarus Man*--and has treated them with close-up intimacy, spurning the expected big action scenes and concentrating on the interactions of very small groups of people. In his fifth and latest novel, however, the treatment meshes harmoniously with the subject, which is his biggest yet.

Like Lawrence Sanders' *The First Deadly Sin*, *Jericho Man* is about a big-city duel between a cop and a maniac. Manhattan is being terrorized by the anonymous Jericho, who several years ago paid nighttime visits to an unknown number of skyscrapers under construction or repair, and planted dynamite in their foundations with scientific precision so that on detonation each building will collapse into its own rubble. In the novel's early chapters Jericho demonstrates his method by destroying a midtown office building, leaving more than 1500 injured or dead. Then he makes his demand in a letter to the mayor: a million dollars within three days or another building implodes. Assigned to track down the madman before time runs out is police captain Dexter Canby, with expert unofficial help from David Strother, the architect of the building Jericho murdered. Political infighting, sexual relationships and the struggles of both Canby and Strother with various forms of guilt are intercut with glimpses of some very wealthy people living wasted lives in another luxury highrise--is one of them Jericho, or is their home the bomber's next target?--as the hours tick away and tension climbs.

Around page 200 Canby suddenly discovers Jericho's identity, which not only comes as a stunning surprise but raises all sorts of interlocking questions about characters' motivations that the final fifty pages, despite full measure of action and confrontation and more surprises, do not really answer. This aside, however, *Jericho Man* is an intricate balance of large-scale disaster, police work, detection and suspense and characterization, an unputdownable page-turner that may well be the best of John Lutz's books to date. (Francis M. Nevins, Jr.)

John Ball. *Then Came Violence*. Doubleday, 1980, 208 pp., $8.95.

With his very first mystery novel, *In the Heat of the Night* (1965), John Ball gave the genre something it sorely needed: an intelligent, dignified black detective, who counteracted earlier stereotypes of blacks much as Earl Derr Biggers' intelligent and dignified Charlie Chan had counteracted 1920s stereotypes of the fiendish Oriental. A rather more earthy and physical version of Ball's homicide investigator Virgil Tibbs was brought to the screen two years later in the person of Sidney Poitier, but the original Mr. Tibbs--cool, totally self-possessed, a lover of fine food and art and classical music--returns every few years in a new detective novel. His sixth and latest book-length adventure may well be his best.

Tibbs comes home to Pasadena from vacation and finds his apartment stripped to the bare walls, but this is only a prelude to his assignment as bodyguard for the disturbingly lovely wife and the two small children of an African head of state who is on the brink of being toppled by guerrillas. Master of concealing his emotions though he is, Tibbs drifts uncontrollably into loving this unattainable woman while at the same time he is confronted with two complex cases: a vicious gang of racially integrated armed robbers, and a vigilante group that seems to be executing violent criminals who slip through the loopholes in the legal system.

In John Ball's world every police officer is a perfect angel--supremely capable, fearsomely honorable, never out of control for a microsecond--and police procedure is an infallible marvel of precision. The supreme virtue is self-possession, never allowing one's true feelings to show, and it is best attained through devotion to the martial arts like karate or aikido. The ceremonial details of eating and drinking reveal to the initiated how one is valued by his peers. A good woman, regardless of her race, serves her man in the manner of a traditional Japanese wife. This Oriental ambience is radically different from the world of Ball's fellow California police novelist Joseph Wambaugh, but the official procedure and jargon are just as accurate in the Tibbs novels, and the police attitudes towards liberal lawyers and judges are identical, although Ball presents them in a characteristically softer key.

Then Came Violence is not terribly satisfactory as a detective story, for we are told nothing about the origins and the ultimate fate of the vigilantes for whom both Tibbs and Ball seem to have a subliminal sympathy, and the deduction by which Tibbs identifies the head of the death squad is nothing short of ludicrous. But in just about every other respect it's a marvelous blend of fast action, emotions, police routine and intellectual sleuthing and a skillful interweaving of three diverse story threads into an integral whole. Readers who have not yet been introduced to the unique fictional world of John Ball can hardly do better than to begin with this novel. (Francis M. Nevins, Jr.)

Roy Harley Lewis. *A Cracking of Spines*. Robert Hale, 1980, 207 pp., Ł5.25.

Ever since Christopher Morley's *The Haunted Bookshop* entered the literary scene in 1919, the bookshop mystery, or one featuring a bookish background, has formed a noteworthy part of the genre.

Although Morley's novel is dated today and was not the first of its kind, it did set the style and tone of what bookshop mysteries should be. Elizabeth Daly, Michael Delving, George Sims, and W. K. Wren each has contributed at least four such novels to this book-oriented category. (I have accumulated over seventy-five myself.) Five additional mysteries--

new this year--could also qualify: Lawrence Block's *The Burglar Who Liked to Quote Kipling*, Robert Barnard's *Death of a Mystery Writer* and *Death of a Literary Widow*, Jonathan Valin's *Final Notice*, and the book at hand, Roy Harley Lewis's *A Cracking of Spines*.

Mr. Lewis's background is certainly promising. He is a practicing bookseller and the author of two books on books: *The Book Browser's Guide* (1975) and *Antiquarian Books: An Insider's Account* (1978). With this knowledge in mind, it stands to reason that all Morley fans should take this inital tome to their collective bosom. Not entirely so, me thinks. *A Cracking of Spines* simply does not fit the Morley mold.

First off, the publisher has done the author an injustice. The proofing is so bad that the reader finds himself looking for the next typo, which is not an aid to one's concentration.

The format is another story. The small 5"x7" size is a real joy. How I wish American publishers would go back to this easily held, lightweight form.

Getting at last to the plot, the protagonist, Matthew Coll, opens a country bookshop on the Devon shore. Housed in a quaint 1703 Queen Anne structure, the shop commands a sixty-mile view of the coastline while still maintaining a Main Street address, surely every bookseller's dream.

But then comes the twist. Coll's previous employment entailed service with Military Intelligence, which leads to his being engaged by the Antiquarian Society to run down a series of rare book thefts. Most of the book concerns itself with the detective rather than bookseller role.

The metamorphosis from meek, mild-mannered bookseller into a man of steel takes our hero first hurdling off into the nearest river, thence to engage the local toughs (three in one page) in appropriate Kung Fu tactics, and finally to encounter an adversary who adopts a Bogie lisp, complete with the following dialog--"Looking for something, sweetheart?" Hardly the sort of chit chat that would drop from the lips of Roger Mifflin.

Clearly, Mr. Lewis did not set out to write another Morley opus. It is only wishful thinking on my part that he should do so. The "gentlemanly profession" has, after all, given way to a vocation more suitably conducted in a K-Mart store.

But while we Morley addicts must suffer this outrageous fortune, it must also be admitted that Roy Lewis can indeed spin a tale of today. The denouement is predictable, but the book is well-plotted, tightly constructed and in book parlance, a "good read."

I look forward to the next Matthew Coll adventure. Who knows, the recession might take its toll and Mr. Coll may have to spend more time in his business. Bookish mysteries are to be encouraged. We "BMFs" must stick together. (R.L. Wenstrup)

Lawrence Sanders. *The Tenth Commandment*. Putnam's, 1980, 385 pp.

Lawrence Sanders has done just about every kind of novel in the field of popular fiction--the crime story in *The Anderson Tapes*, the political thriller in his two books about the man named Tangent, the police procedural in his "Deadly Sin" novels, science fiction in *The Tomorrow File*, the caper book (as

Lesley Andress) in *Caper*, and the private eye story in *The Sixth Commandment*. In the same vein as the latter is *The Tenth Commandment*, which introduces the chief investigator of a New York law firm. The investigator is named Joshua Bigg, and he's 5 feet, 3-3/8 inches tall. That in itself should give you an idea of the style of the book, which introduces another character named Reape--"as in Rook before you Reape." I could go on, but I won't; you get the idea. If you can get past the names, you'll discover Bigg working on two different cases for his firm, both of which no one will be surprised to di-cover are really parts of the same case, which indeed has to do with coveting your neighbor's wife, not to mention his money. There is a murder which looks like suicide and a mysterious disappearance, and Bigg doggedly investigates both until he finds the answer. There's some sharp commentary, and there are some interesting characters. If you've read Sanders before and liked him, you should enjoy this book. (Bill Crider)

Alistair MacLean. *Athabasca*. Doubleday, 1980, 326 pp.

MacLean goes to the frozen north for his subject this time, but without the success of *Night Without End*. We have saboteurs menacing both the Alaskan Pipeline and the oil mines of Athabasca. MacLean gives plenty of technical details and his usual super-agents (named Dermott and MacKenzie this time) and the standard unflappable MacLean bossman, Jim Brady. There's at least one exciting scene, when the giant dragline bears down on Dermott--or was it MacKenzie? With the cardboard characters here, it's hard to tell. And there is some attempt at mystery--why is one finger of a murdered man bent and broken so oddly? But with all this, there's the feeling that MacLean has done it all before, that he's sleepwalking through it. Even the "surprising" revelation at the end fails to surprise. *Athabasca* is finally mediocre MacLean and serves mainly to make one wish that he could write them the way he used to. (Bill Crider)

Nicholas Freeling. *Castang's City*. Pantheon, 1980.

Nicholas Freeling's most recent novel carries a foreword which stipulates that the city is imaginary and "thus has no name; its every feature, and everyone in it, has been brought there by the four winds." And by a very skillfully wielded pen. Emerginf from Freeling's imagination, the city is becoming very real.

The slowly paced plot begins with the terrorist-like murder of Etienne Marcel, a municipal official, and is complicated by the suicide-like murder of his elder son. Richard, Castang, and other members of the Police Judiciare undertake the investigation, a complex, frustrating process. We observe interrogations, surveilance, and staff meetings. These meetings figure very importantly, and the portraits of Castang's professional family--a varied, capable, independent crew-- become far clearer than they have been heretofore.

Families, in fact, are a major motif in this novel. The growing, developing Castang family (their baby is born in the course of the story) is contrasted with the diminishing, disintegrating Marcel family. Both stand for branches of humanity, and the author asks--quietly but intently--where that largest of all families is headed. Freeling's serious doubts about our prospects are marvelously dramatized in the brief, final chapter which depicts Henri and Vera Castang's reactions to the death of Jacques Brel.

Freeling takes a great authorial risk in introducing the Brel symbol so late in the book, but the device works very well. So do the others. The city itself stands for western civilization, and in one stunning image, the villain is depicted as a building:

> No good stone. Brick, and poor quality: once exposed to this sulphuric-acid-laden PJ air it crumbles, at the corners first; faster.... And under the plaster, a smell, smell of damp and decay. The name of this smell is prevarication. (p. 229)

As always in a Freeling novel, the extensions of his observations (from nuclear family to city to nation to western culture) are established and constantly reenforced by telling references to film, fiction, and music. These allusions are usually introduced during the conversations which dominate the book's structure, and prospective readers should be warned that in *Castang's City*, character development is more important than physical action.

Interesting as a study in police procedure, the novel is also an intriguing examination of decent people trying to hold the line against corruption and decay. The Castangs are flawed but sound, brave folk; their latest appearance makes a fine book. (Jane S. Bakerman)

Margaret Yorke. *The Cost of Silence*. Arrow Books, 1977.

Oodles of the inhabitants of Old Bidbury figure importantly in Margaret Yorke's *The Cost of Silence*. Plots and subplots abound, and violence is on the rampage: secrets from the past, thwarted romances, a battered child, rape, a runaway-- and murder. Once again, the old corruption-beneath-the-placid-surface theme is evoked, and once again, it works.

Norman Widnes, the ironmonger, has spent his life caring for invalids, first his mother and now his wife, a woman considerably his senior. When Emma Widnes is murdered, the whole village speculates. Was it a burglar, as it seems, or has Norman rid himself of a gross and dreadful burden in order to marry his mistress, a restless local teacher? Actually, the reader knows the answer, for Yorke has written an inverted mystery and shows us, relentlessly, each step toward the killing. The suspense arises from the suspicion growing around Norman and from hints about the closely guarded secret harbored in his past.

Despite his past and his double life, Norman is a curiously innocent personality. He and Jamie Renshaw, a seven-year-old terrified of dogs, are contrasted with Mick Green and Paula Curtis, characters who were, it seems, born utterly selfish and corrupt. Other pairings are also important as Yorke compares two elderly women coping with loneliness; two young couples, each mismatched; and the adulteries of Norman Widnes and Harry Pearce.

The book is highly episodic, focusing briefly and swiftly on one character, then another. This device demands constant changes in point of view which can, at times, be a problem for the reader--reading it is a little like watching an afternoon soap opera. But by and large, the shifts work acceptably, and Yorke achieves unity by two motifs. One is identified in the title; various characters preserve very costly silences. The second motif operates on a wholly different level; transitions are managed, motivations are generated, and personalities are revealed through the characters' reactions to their dogs--and there are hosts of canines in the village. It's a clever ploy, and, luckily, Yorke keeps it just this side of cuteness. Similarly, she keeps sentimentality under control, largely through the astringency of one of the old ladies, Mrs. Minter, and the tough resolution of Mrs. Pearce. *The Cost of Silence* is one of Margaret Yorke's best efforts. (Jane S. Bakerman)

Stanley Ellin. *The Specialty of the House and Other Stories*. Mysterious Press, 1980, 557 pp., $15.00.

"They are demonstrations of tender loving care for technical perfection, of craftsmanship exercised on every detail, and hang the expense." The quotation is from Stanley Ellin's 1967 story "The Twlefth Statue" and the ostensible subject is the films of Cecil B. DeMille but the description applies even better to the output of Ellin himself. Since his literary debut in 1948 and devoting full time to fiction, he has published an astonishingly small body of work (one dozen novels and three dozen short stories) but one whose every word is patiently shaped and polished until it glistens with perfection. He has won two Edgar awards from the Mystery Writers of America, France's *Grand Prix de Litterature Policiere,* and universal critical acclaim as a prime mover in the evolution of mystery fiction away from the dry deductive puzzle and towards the modern tale of social and psychological and literary quality that happens to be in some sense about crime or criminals.

The Mysterious Press, a small but select Manhattan publishing house (129 West 56th St., New York, NY 10019) specializing in collections of crime short stories, has now assembled in one volume all of Ellin's short fiction from the unforgettable "The Specialty of the House" (1948) to the hauntingly contemporary "Reasons Unknown" (1978). The publisher has thoughtfully printed the date of each story within the running head at the top of every page, so that the reader can set in the correct time context events that today would be ludicrous, for example that the main character in "The Cat's-Paw" (1949) would consent to murder a total stranger in return for a guaranteed $50 a week for life.

Like his peers Roald Dahl and John Collier, and like the late Sir Alfred Hitchcock who frequently used all three authors' tales on his TV series, Ellin tends to take the most hideous subjects--literal and figurative cannibalism, madness, vengeance, fouled relationships, random slaughter--and treat them with cool surgical precision. This collection of his stories celebrates the enduring quality and endless re-readability of one of the masters of quiet cerebral horror. (Francis M. Nevins, Jr.)

George V. Higgins. *Kennedy for the Defense*. Knopf, 1980, 225 pp., $9.95.

    In his early novels like *The Friends of Eddie Coyle* (1972), former Federal prosecutor George V. Higgins portrayed the fringes of the Boston underworld with *cinema verité* authenticity. After a few undistinguished ventures into other fictional territory, Higgins has returned to home turf in his ninth novel in which we see the world through the eyes of a criminal defense lawyer. Jeremiah F. Kennedy, however, is by no means Boston's Perry Mason. He's a paunchy, fortyish family man whose clients are almost invariably guilty and whose function is not to defend these people in court but to make deals for them with other functionaries, getting reduced charges, probation, suspended sentences, whatever he can for his clientele of thieves, pimps, drunk drivers and assorted moral toads. The high fees which he demands for his services and whose sources do not concern him he uses to provide the good life for the wife and teen-age daughter he adores.
    As usual in Higgins novels, this one has no sustained plot but deals with a series of unrelated criminal cases that keep disrupting Kennedy's beach vacation with his family. The clients include a professional car thief who claims a state trooper ate his license and then arrested him for driving without one, the gay son of an obnoxious nabob who was so indiscrete as to proposition an undercover cop, and a hopelessly stupid young mechanic who's being set up for a drug bust by a corrupt FBI agent. In due course the games are played, the deals are made, credible coincidence intertwines some of the cases, there are a couple of bloody shootouts--not described directly but recounted after the fact by Kennedy to his wife or a neighbor--and what we laughingly call the criminal justice system lurches on. Higgins passes no overt moral judgments but is content to let us draw our own conclusions, which may not be as complacent as his protagonist's, from this compulsively readable story, full of the irritations and compromises and unconcise conversations and undeodorized smells of real criminal law practice. It's good to have Higgins back with the kind of book he does best. (Francis M. Nevins, Jr.)

THE DOCUMENTS IN THE CASE
(Letters)

From Charles Shibuk, 2084 Bronx Park, East, Bronx, NY 10462:
   In the past, I've had the privilege of meeting several people who edit the various magazines devoted to the mystery genre.
   This happy state of affaris started in 1967 whe I first met Al Hubin--some five months before he started TAD.
   Two years later, Al introduced me to Bob Briney.
   I attended the Los Angeles Bouchercon in 1976 and met Art Scott.
   The following year I met Jeff Meyerson at the New York Bouchercon.
   I've recently returned from the Bouchercon held in Washington where I've had the (very dubious) honor of making the acquaintance of the peripatetic editor of this journal.
   Unbelievable!
   The man is absolutely wild.
   Therefore, innocent readers of TMF should be warned against seeking this person out at some future date because they admire this magazine--which is so much more interesting than its editor!
   Guy Townsend, I must admit, is quite a character, but paradoxically a really forgettable one. My nightmarish memories of him are rapidly receding as I slowly recover from the experience.
   In all fairness, I should note that his squint is not quite as bad as I had expected.
   However, in spite of all this, I may renew my subscription.
   [*Aw, shucks, Charlie....*]

From Marv Lachman, 34 Yorkshire Dr., Suffern, NY 10901:
   TMF 4:4 awaited me when we returned from Bouchercon. Even without your description in "Mysteriously Speaking" I was able to recognize you in Washington. However, the "squint in one eye" you mention explains why you kept confusing me with my good old Bronx buddy, Charlie Shibuk. All we mystery people with roots in The Bronx, e.g. Edgar Allan Poe, Otto Penzler, Jim McCahery, Charlie Shibuk, and Marv Lachman, Look alike. [*Like clones, every one of them. Honest.*]
   Reading Ellen Nehr on LOM is almost as much fun as listening to her in person. Years ago, in one of my articles, I left out the name of the author of the short story I was discussing. I don't know if it was deliberate, but Ellen omitted the creators of four of her LOM. Qqulleran, Forbes, Evans, and Mayo were created, respectively, by Lilian Jackson Braun, Richard Starnes, Elliot Paul, and Phoebe Atwood Taylor (previously mentioned in the article in connection with her Witherall LOMan).
   Barry Van Tilburg's dossiers of spy series characters continue to be a treasure trove of useful information. Likewise, Steve Lewis's reviews, especially the perceptive (he agreed with me) one of Dick Francis' *Whip Hand*. I also enjoyed Alexandersson and Hedman on Charteris and, especially, Dueren on The Great Merlini.
   The only problem is Lachman's column, "It's About Crime."

I've read all his stuff before....

From Toby Brust, 42 Calhoun Street, Torrington, CT 06790:
   Got back from our trip home to Chicago and found all of Volume 3 waiting for me, for which I am enclosing my check and my thanks.
   I have spent many hours reading these issues and I can't begin to tell you how very much I have enjoyed them. The articles are very good, and contain a lot of information that I ahve been looking for for years. For the first time I do not feel so frustrated at not being able to find what has been written recently by which author. I love Steve's reviews, and through them have found a lot of books I never knew existed. More books that I can buy from him.
   Your Saga on Nero Wolfe is terrifis. I have really enjoyed that. Rex Stout is #2 on my Hit Parade. I go back to the Ellery Queen era. He is still #1. The books are good and I have enjoyed them all these many years. I really wonder just what difference it really makes who wrote them, or helped to write them. The enjoyment is in the reading, the character, the story, and if you enjoyed the book, and it is well written, who cares how many collaborated on its writing? I loved those books and really miss them.
   I also have enjoyed the letters very much. They contain a lot of information for a person like me who lives in a town where mystery books are few and far between. We have a very fine bookstore in town, run by a terrific gentleman, who, until I started calling in orders for mysteries, didn't know these authors existed. We have become good friends, as I suspect all mystery lovers have. (The few of us that there is.) My biggest complaint has always been, that you can't walk into a bookstore and find hardcover mysteries on the shelf. Unless, of course, it has made the Best Seller list. Paperbacks aren't much better. Maybe it's Connecticut. In Chicago, where we were originally frim, it was a lot better. I was able to get a few things when we were back there in August.
   Well, thanks to TMF I found that several of my favorite authors have been busy writing recently. I have also found that there are a lot of books written about the authors themselves that are very good. Books that have made my library even better than before.
   I am looking forward to the next issue. Thanks for letting me become a member of the family.
   [*Thanks for wanting to.*]

From Mike Nevins, 7045 Cornell, University City, MO 63130:
   I vastly enjoyed Ellen Nehr's article on little old men detectives but I thought several of those she chose were neither little nor old enough to belong in the category. One who does, and deserves some attention, is recluse Melville Fairr, who appears in two novels and one short story by Craig Rice under her "Michael Venning" byline.

From Claude Saxon, 152 Eastview, Memphis, TN 38111:
   You are quite right, this does seem to be an especially good issue. Read the Bleiler first, because I always find his introductions in Dover reprints so interesting. I've never had much luck with Dickens, but Bleiler's essay inclines me toward another attempt at *Edwin Drood*. One idea presents

itself from my position of complete Dickensian ignorance: could Bazzard be an alter ego of Datchery? [*If I understand what you are saying, Claude, the same thought occurred to me when I read Ev's article. Like you, I have yet to read the unfinished novel, but it seems to me that many of convincing arguments Ev's presents against Bazzard being Datchery are not reversible--that is, they are not nearly so convincing when used to argue that Datchery is not Bazzard.*]

Ellen Nehr's "Little Old Men ..." provides me with more titles to watch for. I will be looking forward to more of her writings; just wish she would be more careful about including names and publication dates with her descriptions.

Most interesting bio on Leslie Charteris, including much information that was new to me. Coincidentally, I just bought some Detective Classics, a Fiction House reprint pulp, including the March 1931 issue, which contained Charteris's *The Last Hero*.

Looking forward to the next issue. Will try to l.o.c.

From Linda Toole, 147 Somershire Dr., Rochester, NY 14617:

Dynamite issue! I thoroughly enjoyed every article--something I've never been able to say before. Even the reproduction was excellent! I would like to get better acquainted with Ellen Nehr's LOM, to say nothing of Merlini.

E.F. Bleiler's article on Datchery was extremely interesting. It sounds as though there's an entire cottage industry based on this unfinished work. Mr. Bleiler certainly seems to make a good case for Datchery-Drood. The article does, however, cause mixed emotions. Much as I enjoyed it, I hope TMF won't go this route completely. The usual tenor of TMF is cozy-conversational--a discussion among friends; whereas Datchery seems more of an impersonal lecture. From what I know of TAD (and that's not much and third hand) it seems like it wound up as a semi-scholarly magazine--devoid of TMF's warmth.

From Becky Reineke, 1648 Zarthan Ave. S., Minneapolis, MN:

I love it! I love it!

But (groan) four issues at one time? Arrived home from work at 5 p.m. yesterday, emptied the mailbox, buried my nose in TMF and scarcely lifted my eyes until I reluctantly noticed it was 11 p.m. I don't remember making dinner, although my husband insists he ate it. And, of course, my other reading went out the window, even though I'm cramming to vote in Steve's author poll. What have you done to me, Guy? Bless you! I love every page! And Steve will have to wait.

Some news, old by now, still alarmed me. I don't understand the mechanics or reasons involved, but with this last relocation of yours I hope things have quietly settled down. [*Actually, I'm on the run from the law as a result of an unfortunate business scheme of mine involving a duck and a peg-legged dwarf, the details of which I can't go into at this time....*] I can understand the peaks and valleys. Everyone has those no matter what they do for employment or what crazy hobbies they become involved in. But this crazy hobby, reading and collecting, is exactly what has sustained me through my valleys. Frankly, I don't know how you do it. So much effort and enthusiasm and sacrifice (i.e., missing out on some of your own reading) is required. When you moved you should have come Minnesota way, for I stand here willing to lend a hand. I'm still willing. Has your quest for cover art ended? I'm kicking around a few ideas. I love the four covers on this year's issues to date--real panache. [*Of those four covers, two were recycled from earlier issues, which should answer your question as to whether my quest for cover art has ended. Put those ideas you mention down on paper and send them on--preferably camera-ready.*]

Please continue to ignore Jeff Banks and keep printing "The Documents in the Case". I realize there is a size difference of this section between 4:1 and 4:4, but letters should pick up what with summer fading and everyone moving indoors again. (Does it snow in Arkansas? [*Sometimes.*]) Letter section or not, TMF is every inch as professional as the strictly edited zines, and its sense of openness and camaraderie allows it to stand uniquely above all the rest.

It's quite difficult to comment on any one thing when you're overwhelmed with four issues simultaneously. Let me just say that the smattering of reviews and articles I sampled were all excellent and captured my immediate interest. Centering on the most recent issue, 4:4, my favorite piece had to be "The Great Merlini" by Fred Dueren, and I've now entered Rawson, Clayton, to the bottom of my ever-growing reading list. Oh, temptation. I would love to order each and every back issue, but I'm slamming the brakes on here and will progress from the present rather than scurry to get caught up on the past (an impossible feat for me). I hope to see your complete Nero Wolfe Saga in published form in the future....

As you read this, of course, you will have returned from (survived?) the annual Bouchercon. I expect to hear all about in in TMF [*The next issue will be a Bouchercon special*], as I couldn't attend (rats)! There is a rumor floating around that Bouchercon XII is to be held in Milwaukee. If true, I expect I would be able to attend that before travelling all the way to Washington, DC, although I suppose no one else will show up. [*It's true, all right, and you are in for a surprise; Bouchercons in the midwest are well attended by fans from all parts of the country.*]

From David Doerrer, 4626 Baywood Circle, Pensacola, FL 32504:

Jottings from an erratic correspondent who can't blame his lack of response on your nomadic existence.

I have been most pleased by the amount of espionage material in TMF 4:1-4, although I'm sure that someone is going to complain that there has been too much. Ignore them.

4:1--Especially enjoyed the Quiller report and the article on Luard. Nice, meaty letter section. Frank Floyd's were virtually a mini-article in themselves.

4:2--Kudos to Barry Van Tilburg for conceiving, and writing, his dossier series. I hope that this has a long run, which it can easily do if he doesn't run out of steam before he runs out of material. A minor quibble is that I wouldn't call Quiller "non-violent".

In reference to Jim O'Donnell's letter, *The Kobra Manifesto* was published in the U.S. by Doubleday, and reprinted by Dell in 1978. *The Sinkiang Executive* has also been published by Doubleday in 1978, who have also published *The Scorpion Signal* this year, with the pb to Playboy Press.

Apologies to all your readers for the margins on the

"Index". Had I But Known that it would not be typeset, I would have made allowances. [*The fault is mine, David, for not telling you.*]

Also very pleased to see Jeff Banks' chart on Modesty Blaise, who is becoming one of my favorite women, next to Diana Rigg, of course. Some time back, Art Scott (who knows of my affection for Modesty) sent a copy of *Comic Media*'s special Modesty Blaise issue which has a long--and very well done--interview with Peter O'Donnell. In the course of this, O'Donnell mentions that the comic strips flopped in the U.S. and that he had been "told that it was too sophisticated for the American market"! Times have apparently changed--the interview was done, or at least appeared, in 1973--for I was pleasantly surprised to find the morning daily paper in Rochester, New York, carrying it this summer. They didn't have it a year ago. In addition to the interview, there was a short strip--never before published--on Modesty's origins and all-too-brief segments from two other stories. Star Books has published the first two strips in a pb entitled *Modesty Blaise in the Beginning* (1978) and *Modesty Blaise: The Black Pearl & The Vikings* (n.d.). According to a recent publishers list which I got from George Kelley, the following are all in print from Pan Books (London): *Dragon's Claw*, *I, Lucifer*, *Last Day in Limbo*, *Modesty Blaise*, *Sabre Tooth*, *The Silver Mistress* and *A Taste for Death*, leaving only *The Impossible Virgin* and *Pieces of Modesty* currently o.p., unless I've missed some.

Michael Jayston is currently playing Peter Guillam in *Tinker, Tailor, Soldier, Spy*, and I would have loved to see him as Quiller. George Segal didn't impress me at all in *The Quiller Memorandum*; too wise-guy.

4:3--I really hate to disagree with Theodore Dukeshire, as we both obviously enjoy spy stories, but I just can't go along with Vladimir Gull as a successor to James Bond. In the first place, Gull isn't an agent. In addition, he doesn't understand, and hates, guns, and wasn't terribly competent in the first two books.

For Karen LaPorte, who would like me to "be a little more polite" and "get all the facts first" in my comment:

I don't believe that I can oblige the lady, for her first admonition is a matter of opinion and her second is meaningless, for only two of my comments were stated as "facts", and they require no support. A "catalogue" is a "list", according to my *Webster's New Collegiate Dictionary*, and I had received two of hers. A difference in choice of terminology is not a question of fact. In remarking on the quality of her selections and on her prices, I deliberately used "seems" and "seem" because these were--and are--opinions. I did not presume to state--as a matter of fact--that her selections were or were not good, merely that they appeared to me to be good ones. As she said, this is "a matter of taste". This was intended as a positive observation; obviously it was not taken as such. Finally, her explanation of costs, mark-up and shipping policies, though interesting, is irrelevant to my comment on her asking price for *The Green Ripper*. This too was an opinion, and we are all entitled to hold--and voice--those.

4:4--Something for everyone--LOMs, spys, Dickens, magicians, and The Saint.

For what it's worth, one man's opinion on the future of TMF: (And these thoughts really didn't begin to coalesce until

I reread the last four issues.) I don't see where a standard cover would detract from the quality. In fact, if you used the one from 3:3, you'd have a really good one. The price of every thing is going to go up, not down, so even a raise to $12.00 might not keep you in the black for too long. I wouldn't object to xerox or mimeo in 8½x11 size if this would enable you to save enough to find a typist, though I'd prefer you didn't switch in the middle of a volume. In short, I'd rather see a more modest--in terms of production costs--TMF than no TMF.

If you do decide to fold your tent at the end of this volume, I'll be doing the "Index to Book Reviews" for my own convenience, and will be happy to furnish a copy to any of your subscribers who would like one, at my cost plus postage.

U.S. POSTAL SERVICE
STATEMENT OF OWNERSHIP, MANAGEMENT AND CIRCULATION
(Required by 39 U.S.C. 3685)

1. TITLE OF PUBLICATION	A. PUBLICATION NO.	2. DATE OF FILING
The Mystery Fancier	4 2 8 5 9 0	3 November 1980

3. FREQUENCY OF ISSUE	A. NO. OF ISSUES PUBLISHED ANNUALLY	B. ANNUAL SUBSCRIPTION PRICE
Bi-monthly	6	$9.00

4. COMPLETE MAILING ADDRESS OF KNOWN OFFICE OF PUBLICATION *(Street, City, County, State and ZIP Code) (Not printers)*

Guy M. Townsend, 840 E. Main St., #5, Blytheville, AR 72315 (Mississippi County)

5. COMPLETE MAILING ADDRESS OF THE HEADQUARTERS OR GENERAL BUSINESS OFFICES OF THE PUBLISHERS *(Not printers)*

Same

6. FULL NAMES AND COMPLETE MAILING ADDRESS OF PUBLISHER, EDITOR, AND MANAGING EDITOR *(This item MUST NOT be blank)*

PUBLISHER *(Name and Complete Mailing Address)*

Same

EDITOR *(Name and Complete Mailing Address)*

Same

MANAGING EDITOR *(Name and Complete Mailing Address)*

Same

7. OWNER *(If owned by a corporation, its name and address must be stated and also immediately thereunder the names and addresses of stockholders owning or holding 1 percent or more of total amount of stock. If not owned by a corporation, the names and addresses of the individual owners must be given. If owned by a partnership or other unincorporated firm, its name and address, as well as that of each individual must be given. If the publication is published by a nonprofit organization, its name and address must be stated.) (Item must be completed)*

FULL NAME	COMPLETE MAILING ADDRESS
Guy M. Townsend (sole owner)	840 E. Main St., #5, Blytheville, AR 72315

8. KNOWN BONDHOLDERS, MORTGAGEES, AND OTHER SECURITY HOLDERS OWNING OR HOLDING 1 PERCENT OR MORE OF TOTAL AMOUNT OF BONDS, MORTGAGES OR OTHER SECURITIES *(If there are none, so state)*

FULL NAME	COMPLETE MAILING ADDRESS
None	

9. FOR COMPLETION BY NONPROFIT ORGANIZATIONS AUTHORIZED TO MAIL AT SPECIAL RATES *(Section 411.3, DMM only)*
The purpose, function, and nonprofit status of this organization and the exempt status for Federal income tax purposes *(Check one)*

☐ (1) HAS NOT CHANGED DURING PRECEDING 12 MONTHS ☐ (2) HAS CHANGED DURING PRECEDING 12 MONTHS *(If changed, publisher must submit explanation of change with this statement.)*

10. EXTENT AND NATURE OF CIRCULATION	AVERAGE NO. COPIES EACH ISSUE DURING PRECEDING 12 MONTHS	ACTUAL NO. COPIES OF SINGLE ISSUE PUBLISHED NEAREST TO FILING DATE
A. TOTAL NO. COPIES (Net Press Run)	350	350
B. PAID CIRCULATION 1. SALES THROUGH DEALERS AND CARRIERS, STREET VENDORS AND COUNTER SALES	0	0
2. MAIL SUBSCRIPTION	152	180
C. TOTAL PAID CIRCULATION (Sum of 10B1 and 10B2)	152	180
D. FREE DISTRIBUTION BY MAIL, CARRIER OR OTHER MEANS SAMPLES, COMPLIMENTARY, AND OTHER FREE COPIES	12	12
E. TOTAL DISTRIBUTION (Sum of C and D)	164	192
F. COPIES NOT DISTRIBUTED 1. OFFICE USE, LEFT OVER, UNACCOUNTED, SPOILED AFTER PRINTING	186	158
2. RETURN FROM NEWS AGENTS	0	0
G. TOTAL (Sum of E, F1 and 2 - should equal net press run shown in A)	350	350

11. I certify that the statements made by me above are correct and complete

SIGNATURE AND TITLE OF EDITOR, PUBLISHER, BUSINESS MANAGER OR OWNER

[signature] Editor

PS Form 3526 (Page 1)
June 1980

(See Instruction on reverse)

www.ingramcontent.com/pod-product-compliance
Lightning Source LLC
Chambersburg PA
CBHW031434040426
42444CB00006B/812